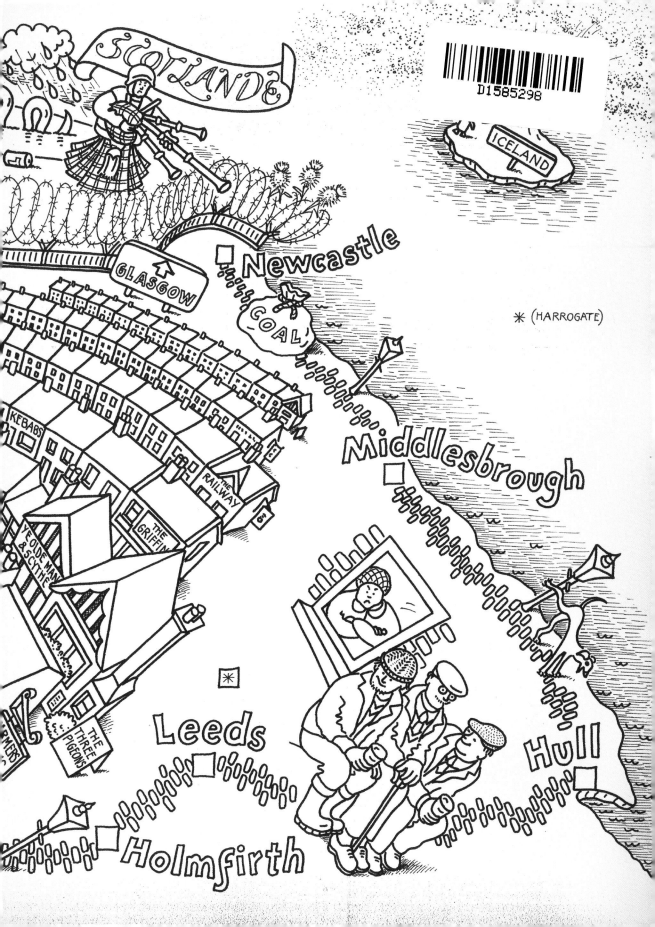

My Guide To The North

My Guide
To The North

(and Scotland & Wales, oh, and less

important places i.e. the south)

By

Paddy McGuinness

HODDER &
STOUGHTON

First published in Great Britain in 2010 by Hodder & Stoughton
An Hachette UK company

Copyright © Paddy McGuinness 2010

The right of Paddy McGuinness to be identified as the Author of the Work
has been asserted by him in accordance with the Copyright, Designs and
Patents Act 1988.

A CIP catalogue record for this title is available from the **British Library**.

ISBN 978 0 340 99834 2

Typeset in Caecilia by **UNREAL-UK.COM**

Printed and bound by Rotolito Lombarda Spa, Italy

Hodder & Stoughton policy is to use papers that are natural, renewable
and recyclable products and made from wood grown in sustainable
forests. The logging and manufacturing processes are expected to
conform to the environmental regulations of the country of origin.

Hodder & Stoughton Ltd
338 Euston Road
London NW1 3BH

www.hodder.co.uk

Dedicated to
Mum, Angie
&
Tony "Tucker" Tobin

Contents

Dear Publisher,

My name is Paddy McGuinness. I am applying for the job of book author. I'm aware that you haven't actually advertised this position, but I thought that if you lot are giving Jordan a book deal, then you must be pretty desperate for authors. That is why I am sending out this speculative CV.

Being totally up front with you, I'm not that good at spelling or diction. But then again, that hasn't stopped Jordan, has it? I should also say that I haven't got that much to write about. Though, as before, ditto Jordan.

My key skills are punctuality, time-keeping and never being late. I look forward to your response.

Yours sincerely,

Paddy McGuinness

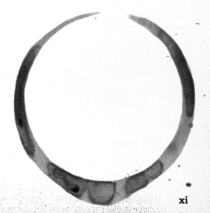

MY C.V.

EDUCATION

(ON AND OFF
FROM 1984?–89?)

MOUNT ST JOSEPH'S, BOLTON
At school, my academic talents were recognised early on. In fact, I was so good they sometimes put me in a class with other special kids. By the end of my school life, at the age of fifteen, I became the most qualified person in my class when I earned two GCSEs in Woodwork and Religious Education.

(BOLTON METROPOLITAN COLLEGE)
BTEC 1st DIPLOMA SCIENCE
I spent two and half years studying for my BTEC with the aim of becoming a Lab Technician. However, the moment I completed the course, I suddenly realised that Lab Technicianary wasn't for me (in fact, I'd rather lick piss off a nettle). By completing the course I demonstrated that I am not a quitter, but by not going on to become a Lab Technician I suppose it does also highlight that I have a low boredom threshold. That attribute might not be so good when it comes to book writing. For example, you wouldn't want me getting bored and finishing mid-sente

OTHER QUALIFICATIONS

- Cycling Proficiency Test: Pass
- 10m Front Crawl Certificate
- 10m Front Crawl Badge
- STD Clinic Check: Pass

WORK EXPERIENCE

(1991)

BRABBIN & RUDD'S, BOLTON – WAREHOUSE WORKER

While working at B&R my primary responsibility was working in the warehouse. I picked up skills there which are sure to come in useful should you employ me to become an author, such as reading and forklift truck driving.

(1992)

WARBURTONS MILL, BOLTON – MACHINE CLEANER
The pinnacle of my career to date came at Warburtons where I worked as a Machine Cleaner. That dough doesn't clean itself off those machines, you know! Turns out you have to painstakingly scrape it off in an unnaturally warm environment, while being scrutinised constantly by foremen, who were only in charge because they'd worked there the longest, so felt it was their right to order young lads about. If that wasn't enough, you also had the life sucked out of you by a constant humming of the machines, lack of daylight and a yearning to lick piss off a nettle. There was an upside; you could buy a loaf for 10p, which was less than half of your wage.

(1994)

VIBROPLANT, BOLTON – YARDMAN
My responsibilities included keeping the yard in order, fixing pneumatic drills, steam cleaning machinery and going for the butties at break time. All relevant skills when it comes to writing a book, I'm sure you'll agree.

(1996)

CLUB 18–30, CORFU – REP
At Club 18–30 my job title was 'Rep', which is short for... well, actually, I don't know what it's short for. Anyway, this role taught me how to interact with drunk, disorderly and desperately randy young folk, while trying to extract money from them. See my earlier Jordan refs.

(YEARS 1997–1999)

HORWICH SWIMMING & FITNESS EMPORIUM, BOLTON – LIFEGUARD & MORE
My time at Horwich Swimming & Fitness Emporium allowed me to demonstrate my incredible versatility. During my employment there, I took on the roles of lifeguard, duty manager, fitness instructor, resource officer, receptionist, bin technician and cleaner. I am proud to say that no one died on my watch as a lifeguard, but there was the odd turd in the pool.

PRESENT

(1999–2010)

Miscellaneous telly stuff.

FAMiLY PHOTOS

MY FAMILY

November '81. Here I am with the family. As you can tell, I bear a striking resemblance to a young Burt Reynolds. But a lot of people say I've got my father's eyes.

ME

SACK RACE

January '82. The only thing I've ever won was the sports day sack race. My dad saw that this was my greatest talent and so trained me for the next nine years until, in '91, he was informed that there was no such thing as professional sack racing.

ON THE BEACH

July '83. This was one of the hottest days on record in the North, so everyone went down the beach. Later that day me and my friend went rock pooling with a bucket, a chisel and an ice pick.

SCHOOL PLAY

December '83. This is where I first trod the boards. My first taste of the limelight – the school nativity. I played the king. I must say, the other kings had some weird ideas about how Elvis dressed.

DOWN THE PUB

January '82. It was quite easy to get served at our local if you were under-age. On the one hand we were breaking the law, on the other hand the bar was always full. So who's the real loser in that situation? I suppose technically it was Al the barman when he got that whopping fine for serving minors – but you get what I'm saying.

SCHOOL YEAR PHOTO

March '83. Admittedly I was held back a few years. But I eventually got my head round the basics... reading, writing and talking.

10TH BIRTHDAY

August '83. My parents always thought I should learn a trade. It may not have been the Action Man I wanted, but I shouldn't really complain as I got over 900 presents that year – and my parents got a brand-new extension.

10TH BIRTHDAY PARTY

August '83. My folks always shunned the classic party games, like pass the parcel, and invented their own. Oh, the fun we had.

CHRISTMAS

Christmas '83. If there's one thing you can say about my parents, it's that they're persistent.

Paddy's Family Tree

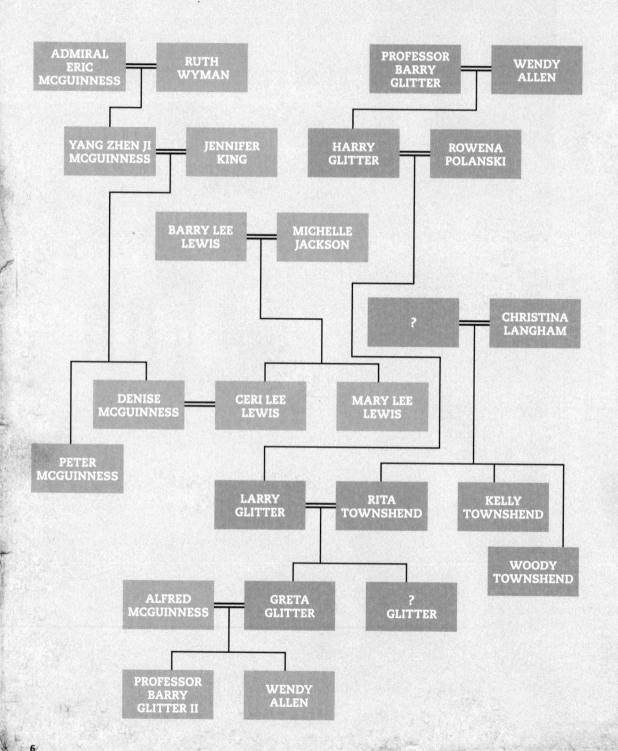

ADMIRAL ERIC McGUINNESS ══ RUTH WYMAN

PROFESSOR BARRY GLITTER ══ WENDY ALLEN

YANG ZHEN JI McGUINNESS ══ JENNIFER KING

HARRY GLITTER ══ ROWENA POLANSKI

BARRY LEE LEWIS ══ MICHELLE JACKSON

? ══ CHRISTINA LANGHAM

DENISE McGUINNESS ══ CERI LEE LEWIS

MARY LEE LEWIS

PETER McGUINNESS

LARRY GLITTER ══ RITA TOWNSHEND

KELLY TOWNSHEND

WOODY TOWNSHEND

ALFRED McGUINNESS ══ GRETA GLITTER

? GLITTER

PROFESSOR BARRY GLITTER II

WENDY ALLEN

ADMIRAL ERIC MCGUINNESS
Naval Officer

Although Eric called himself 'Admiral Eric' and wore an Admiral's hat, he was not actually an Admiral. But this was only discovered after four years at sea, when he was court-martialled for punching an officer after misinterpreting the word 'anchor'.

RUTH WYMAN
Washer Woman

Ruth apparently came from a long line of unemployed musicians but, to her father's disgust, she broke the family tradition when she followed her dreams and became a washer woman.

PROFESSOR BARRY GLITTER
University Lecturer

Barry got a PhD in 'Advanced Canary Deaths' before staying on to teach 'Methods of Coal Reclaiming' at Manchester University. His paper 'How Dirty Coal Can Get' is very well regarded by experts in the field.

WENDY ALLEN
Washer Woman

Wendy is regarded as one of Bolton's first feminists. There was a huge outcry from the community when she became the first female to take the role of 'washer woman'. Until this time, all washer women had been men.

YANG ZHEN JI MCGUINNESS
Miner

Yang was a traditionalist. When he wasn't down the mine, he would be down the pub. And when he wasn't down the pub, he was sat at home in his string vest, reading the paper and shouting abuse at the wall.

JENNIFER KING
Baker

Very little historical evidence exists about Jennifer, but I did find some etchings in an old mine. According to this text, her buns were famous in the region, as were her large baps, and a couple of people mention getting a cream horn from her. That's how I know she was a baker.

HARRY GLITTER
C.E.O.

Harry owned a string of subterranean fuel-picking companies. They specialised in the acquisition and collection of black rocks.

ROWENA POLANSKI
Ballet Dancer

Rowena was one of the greatest dancers to come out of Bolton. She specialised in playing roles of everyday women such as mothers, housewives and washer women.

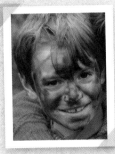

BARRY LEE LEWIS
Miner

Barry's interest in mining started at the age of three. His parents were very encouraging and helped him to live the dream by putting him to work in the mine that year.

MICHELLE JACKSON
Housewife

Michelle dedicated her life to looking after her children. Her favourite hobby was washing and drying clothes.

CHRISTINA LANGHAM
Unknown

We managed to unearth this photo of her with a bucket, some water and some clothes. But we wouldn't like to speculate about what she did for a living without more information.

PETER MCGUINNESS
King of Siberia

(Sources need to be verified) According to his own journal (which does smell a bit of urine and meths), Peter has an impressive CV. From working in a mail room, he moved on to become chef to Winston Churchill's dogs, after which he became the first female captain of the QE2 and eventually was crowned King of Siberia. He also claims to have invented chips and triangles.

DENISE MCGUINNESS
Washer Woman

Denise had a terrible careers adviser.

CERI LEE LEWIS
Miner

Ceri decided to take on the family business. Like her father, she was passionate about her job and got a scholarship to Burnley Girls School for Sub-Surface Miners.

MARY LEE LEWIS
Wisher Woman

Records suggest she was a wisher woman, but I think that might be a spelling mistake.

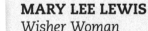

LARRY GLITTER
Doctor

Dr Glitter specialised in diseases of the lungs. He pioneered medical techniques for prolonging the life of miners, such as sucking on coal to acclimatise your lungs to coal dust. His alternative 'coal dust snorting' technique didn't catch on as much.

RITA TOWNSHEND
Writer

Townshend wrote a lot of books on the subject of cleaning clothes, and also about the extraction of coal from coal faces. No one knows where she got her influences from, but then she did always pride herself in thinking outside the box.

KELLY TOWNSHEND (aka Our Kelly)
Mad Cat Lady

Kelly loved cats so much that she started to collect them, both alive and dead. She should have made it into the Guinness Book of Records for having the most cats, but they were too scared to go over to her house because of the screaming.

WOODY TOWNSHEND
Drunk

Woody held the position of Town Drunk for twenty-two years before he was made redundant in 1963 when a government inquiry revealed that the position might be considered 'irresponsible' by some. Woody was going to stage a one-man protest. But forgot.

ALFRED MCGUINNESS
Miner

Alfred always believed in doing a good, honest, hard day's work. But only once a week. The rest of the week he'd call in sick and have a flutter down the bookies.

GRETTA GLITTER
Washer Woman

Gretta was enamoured with her mother's writings and was influenced so much by the subject matter of her books that Gretta became a washer woman. This move was highly unexpected by many in the local community.

? GLITTER
Singer

We now believe that Gretta had a brother who none of the family spoke about. Although most information points to him being a singer, there is also evidence that he might also have been involved with miners.

MARTIN MCGUINNESS
Politician

Martin moved to Ireland at a young age where he easily integrated into the local community by joining lots of clubs and groups. Always very passionate about his hobbies. He is now a politician. Strangely, he no longer mentions his English family ties.

PADDY MCGUINNESS
Comedian/Philosopher

The youngest, most attractive and most intelligent member of the McGuinness family. Although he enjoys telling eloquent and humorous tales on the big stage, he sees comedy as a stepping stone towards a career in long wall mining.

HOW TO TELL IF YOU'RE NORTHERN:
Do you live in a house like this?

I know what some people are thinking when they read this. They're thinking, 'Paddy, with this so-called book of yours, you're just perpetuating the non-existent North–south divide in Britain and using it to reinforce outdated stereotypes and old-fashioned clichés that are no longer relevant, useful or wanted.'

But I'm a modern man, me – and I know when the time has come to break down those age-old cultural barriers. I know it's time to move our thinking into the 21st century, to turn over a new leaf and start afresh. And I also know that this page of the book isn't the time or the place to do any of that. So let's get back to the matter in hand, shall we?

If you're still unsure as to where you come from, another way to tell if you are a Northerner or not is to have a look around your house. Go on, do it right now! Or, if you're reading this at work in your factory tea break or whatever, have a look when you get home. These are the key indicators to look for in your home to discover if you're Northern or not.

COAL SCUTTLE

If you don't own a coal scuttle, you're southern. If your coal scuttle is copper-coloured, buffed to a high shine and contains golf umbrellas, walking poles or squash racquets – you're southern. If your coal scuttle is used for storing back issues of *Country Life, Harper's Bazaar or Horse & Hound* – you're southern. And if you've got any sort of decorative houseplant growing out of it, you're southern. If, however, your coal scuttle contains coal – give yourself a pat on the back; you're Northern.

FLOORING

Does the flooring in your house consist of Scotchguarded, velvet pile, royal blue Axminster carpet that costs more per metre than rope made from unicorns' eyebrows? Does it resemble a game of Tetris where every bit is the same colour and made from endangered Tanzanian mpingo wood neatly slotted together, sanded smooth and varnished eight times? Do you pad about on a Persian rug emblazoned with your own family crest? If you answered 'Yes' to any of the above, you're a southerner. Even a floor of tarmac is considered distinctly southern. True Northerners prefer a traditional cobble throughout.

TV

HD, 1080p, LCD, 42in... these are all just meaningless letters and numbers. Never mind flat-screens and plasmas, proper Northerners want a robust, Bakelite telly with one speaker, two buttons and three channels. Any hint of Channel 4 or a remote control being present are telltale signs you're in a southerner's house. Don't even get me started on Channel 5!

CARD-PLAYING DOGS

This is proper art. A timeless classic. As are the ducks. No twigs, clip frames, crap photography or splodges of paint here. For more on this – turn to page 210 for the Northern Guide to Art.

ODOUR

Now, you can't see this, so I'm going to tell you instead. A Northern house smells of fresh bread, coal, and hard graft. Nothing else. No lavender-scented plug-ins, no jasmine- and cedarwood-flavoured candles, no Shake'n'Vac and no exotic food smells (i.e. croissants, chicken kiev or gingerbread latte). Be warned: you might walk into a southern house that *looks* Northern – but it's important to check: does it *smell* Northern?

TOILET

It's not so much an 'en-suite' as just outside. This goes a long way to maintaining the 'odour' element of a Northern property as described elsewhere on this page. And as an aside – quilted, scented or coloured toilet paper is a sure-fire sign you're in a southern house. In fact, any sort of toilet roll is a sure-fire sign you're in a southern house. Northerners have always preferred bits of ripped-up newspapers threaded on to a string. There, see – recycling. Another great invention for which the North doesn't get the recognition it deserves.

MANCHESTER

HISTORY

Manchester was originally formed by a tribe of Celtics. These natives were known for their large 'Moobs' (or 'Man Chests' as they were known back then). Hence the name 'Manchester'. The city was built next to the capital of the North – Bolton. Why? Well, the Celtics didn't want students going into the holy land (Bolton), and taking over their sacred temples (pubs). So Manchester was created as a sort of student trap – a kind of decoy to keep the dreadlocked free-loading monkeys away. And to this day, not one student has ever entered Bolton.

Manchester is well known for its musical and social influences – from Oasis and Ian McShane to Bernard Manning, this city has become a shining beacon of culture on the international map. Many people of historical note visited Manchester for its cosmopolitan nightlife.

> 'The only thing we have to fear is fear itself nameless, unreasoning, unjustified terror which paralyses needed efforts to convert retreat into advance. What I'm saying is, you talk so hip, man, you're twisting my melon, man.'
>
> Franklin D. Roosevelt, while off his mash on salmon

In the 1st century General Agricola (doesn't sound like a local lad) ordered the construction of a fort. Although, if he was a true Manc, he would have

NORTH

SCOTLAND

Manchester

WALES

OTHER LESS IMPORTANT PLACES (IE. THE SOUTH)

seen the quotes the builders gave him, decided to get the parts himself, and then build it with his Uncle Mick who reckoned he knew a 'fair bit' about forts.

Anyway, to cut a long story short, cotton was made there and then Manchester United started.

ATTRACTIONS

• **GAY VILLAGE** As the name suggests, this is the happiest part of Manchester. And no wonder they're happy – there's almost always a carnival on there! I love a carnival! Everyone in the Gay Village knows how to have fun. Just last night I saw a man there dressed in women's clothing... it were funny as! They've got such a great sense of humour them lads. The guys down there must also be keen on their holidays as my mate mentioned that they do a lot of cottaging. That'll explain why they're so laid back. If you have time, definitely come and check out Manchester's happiest village.

NOTE: Like most tourist destinations, there is a dark side. Certain bars are frequented by rough bikers or Hell's Angels. They're all dressed in leather and chains with handle bar moustaches, you can't miss them.

• **GRANADA STUDIOS TOUR** (closed) Just imagine a place where you can go to see 10 Downing Street (closed), Baker Street (closed) and Checkpoint Charlie (closed) all in one place! Well, Granada has replicas of them all! There's a set in which the furniture has been made massive to give the illusion that you're very small (closed) – it's amazing! Or why not fly like Superman on their green screen (because it's closed)? Or feel like you're part of

the Aliens film in the motion cinema (closed)? It's a great day out for family and friends, I can highly recommend it.

I should also mention that this attraction is now closed but there is a light at the end of the tunnel. The Jeremy Kyle Show is filmed there.

NOTE: The light at the end of the tunnel can be misconstrude as hell on earth.

• **CURRY MILE** Wilmslow Road is home to over seventy Indian restaurants in one mile. But with so much choice, which are the pick of these restaurants? Well, I've had many a meal on the Curry Mile and so thought I'd share my favourites with you. Here's my pick of the crop:

5. Jade Garden Chinese Restaurant
It has a great atmosphere and lovely food – I recommend the sweet & sour – it's fantastic.

4. The Battered Cod
This is a gem. You genuinely won't find better battered fish anywhere else on the Curry Mile. ⟫→

3. Casa Tapas
I think this is the perfect example of the sort of food available on the Curry Mile.

2. The Italian Job
Good old pasta and pizza done to perfection!

1. Spice Hut Indian Restaurant
Now this is more like it! A Curry Mile classic. But read the menu thoroughly, so you don't miss out on their more exciting dishes. For example, they do a great European peppered steak. But, obviously, if you were thinking of something more adventurous, then why not try their Spanish Omelette?

• **FERNANDO'S** The Jewel in Manchester's social crown. This is the hottest nightspot in Manchester. All the biggest celebs have been through its doors, because the owner stole said doors from a skip outside London's Ivy restaurant. Whatever you do, make sure you book early if you want to be guaranteed a seat. It doesn't get busy, it's just that they only have six seats (they used to have more but they keep getting smashed in barfights). Nevertheless, it's the ideal place to go for a boogie, and the dance floor is always full. Largely because they keep forgetting to put the bin bags out and the dance floor's the only place they can store them.

FAMOUS MANCUNIANS

• **JOHN THAW** Best known for stabbing his home city in the back by starring in the Oxford-based drama, Inspector Morse. Come on now, which city has the most crimes? Oxford or Manchester? What is there to investigate in Oxford? Who didn't get their 'prep' in on time? Whether someone cheated in a game of 'Lacrosse'? No. Morse should have been filmed up here where we have proper crimes like mugging, vandalism and Jeremy Kyle's audience!

• **LIAM GALLAGHER** Liam Gallagher is a local musician from a little band you may have heard of – 'The Rain'. For the few of you who haven't heard of them, they played quite a lot round our way in 1990. You must have seen their posters. They were everywhere. I assume it was the same round the rest of the country. I don't know where the rest of them are now, but Liam started playing in a new band with a family member and moved to London. He's dead to us now.

• **TIMMY MALLETT** Timmy rose to fame by hitting children with a mallet. I think he got the idea from the famous tramp Father Pissedmass, who can often be seen chasing children with hammers. 'Timmy Mallett' is not his real name, it's actually 'Timmy Gunn'. He had to change his name after discovering that the kids' game he invented, 'Gunn's Gun', didn't go down too well with the parents. Where is he now? That's a question his family often ask... because he's always trying to be funny by hiding in cupboards. Mallett was last spotted with eighties chart topper David Van Day, eating kangeroos' dicks, in Australia.

PUBLIC HOLIDAYS

• **4-HOUR PARTY PEOPLE DAY** On this day, everyone who used to party 24 hours in the late eighties goes out clubbing – but now everyone's got kids so they need to be home earlier. And rather than getting ripped to the tits on charlie, everyone gets pleasantly full of salad. And as the Hacienda doesn't exist any more, it now takes place in the 'Ask' pasta and pizza restaurant.

• **HOLLYWOOD DAY** Sadly, for the people of Los Angeles, Manchester is twinned with Los Angeles. On Hollywood Day both cities celebrate their extensive similarities. These include: David Beckham. Universal Studios/The Corrie set. The fact that they both have airports... and nothing else, unless you include gang warfare.

LOCAL TRIVIA

• The Wheel of Manchester is better than the London Eye.

• Manchester's tram system was voted number 1 in a recent poll of most dangerous road dangers.

• Manchester Piccadilly is better than London Piccadilly.

• Manchester's burglars are officially the most friendly law-breakers in the UK.

• Velvet Goldmine are named after Manchester's famous velvet goldmine.

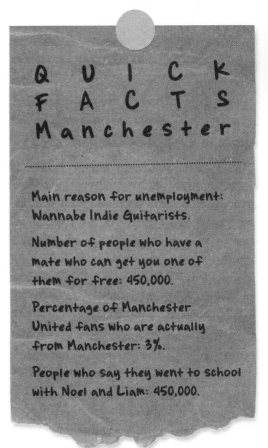

QUICK FACTS Manchester

Main reason for unemployment: Wannabe Indie Guitarists.

Number of people who have a mate who can get you one of them for free: 450,000.

Percentage of Manchester United fans who are actually from Manchester: 3%.

People who say they went to school with Noel and Liam: 450,000.

LIVERPOOL

HISTORY

In 1207, King John – the sovereign of England – officially announced the creation of the Borough of Liverpool. The citizens rejoiced in the streets at this royal recognition. With the ceremony over, King John returned to his horse only to find it standing on bricks with its horseshoes removed.

Liverpool grew to become a dominant city in the fields of industry, sport and culture. William Shakespeare himself originally set his play *Richard III* in Liverpool, only to change the location in subsequent manuscripts:

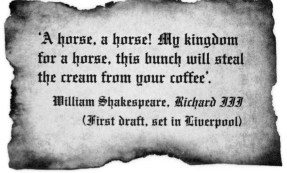

'A horse, a horse! My kingdom for a horse, this bunch will steal the cream from your coffee'.

William Shakespeare, *Richard III*
(First draft, set in Liverpool)

Then, in the middle of the 1900s, Liverpool became the birthplace of a global cultural phenomenon – an act so influential the whole world would sit up and listen. Yes, you know what I'm talking about – Derek Acorah was born. The voice of Thomas the Tank Engine, Ringo Starr, also comes from Liverpool.

SCOTLAND

NORTH

Liverpool

WALES

OTHER LESS IMPORTANT PLACES

(IE. THE SOUTH)

CULTURE

Liverpool was the European Capital of Culture in 2008. You may laugh but when you look into it, a fair few cultural heavyweights have come out of this city.

Of course, when you mention 'Liverpool', there is one group of musicians that immediately springs to mind; a bunch of lads who changed the world with their wonderful music and became international legends. So it's only fitting that I start things off with them:

• **The Royal Liverpool Philharmonic Orchestra**
These guys play all your favourite classical tunes. From the one that sounds like the *Champions League* theme tune, to the one off the old Hovis advert, from the one that they use at the start of the *X Factor* to the one from that space film. They can turn their violins, oboes and bassoons to anything.

• *Brookside/Phil Redmond*
Brookside was a living sculpture by artist Phil Redmond, which was exhibited between 1982 and 2003. A giant, life-size replica of a suburban street was built as the performance space and Redmond filled this arena with talented performance artists such as Ricky Tomlinson, Claire Sweeney and Simon O'Brien. This living, breathing, social experiment was filmed twenty-four hours a day and highlights were broadcast on Channel 4 in the evenings and in a Sunday omnibus. A spin-off show called *Big Brother* was launched by Channel 4 in 2000.

• **Wings** You might have heard of this pop group – and for a very good reason! One of their members used to be in a little band you'll know called The Moody Blues. That's right, I'm talking about Denny Laine, who was the guitarist and singer in Wings and, along with a couple of others, went on to record such smash hits as 'Live and Let Die', 'Jet' and 'Band on the Run'. ≫→

LANDMARKS

• **Fred's Weather Map** I'll be totally honest with you on this one. Christ knows if it's still there but if Fred's Weather Map is still bobbing up and down in Albert Dock, it's definitely worth a look. 'Cos if you go there, it means you can basically visit the whole of Britain in one go. Be warned though, I seem to remember it's a bit slippy around the Cotswolds and the odd streaker has been known to run past.

• **The Cavern Club** You can't visit Liverpool without a pilgrimage to the legendary Cavern Club. Back in the sixties, this dingy little cellar played host to some of the greats – The Rolling Stones, The Who and, of course, who can forget the fab four, those cheeky moptops, The Kinks.

• **Anfield** When it comes to sporting venues, nothing on earth compares to the atmosphere created within Anfield. The sporting history that has been created in this amphitheatre is breathtaking. Memorable sporting moments from Anfield include the boxing world featherweight title bout between Freddie Miller and Nelson Tarleton in 1934 and the exhibition tennis match between Fred Perry and Bill Tilden. And of course there are undoubtedly more great sporting moments to come at this wonderful venue, because Anfield will be hosting matches in the 2015 Rugby World Cup.

• **Knotty Ash** Ken Dodd's so-called mythical land of candy cane lampposts, diddy men and jam butty mines actually exists. Granted, Doddy has used a bit of artistic licence with his descriptions. The diddy men wear hoodies, the jam butty mines are big Al's greasy spoon and the candy cane lampposts have all been nicked.

PUBLIC HOLIDAYS

• **Champions' Borrowing Day** An autumn/winter tradition. Every other week on Tuesdays and Wednesdays, Liverpool's wealthy sportsmen generously leave to compete in foreign countries so that fellow Scousers can descend on their homes and borrow their possessions.

• **Firework Night** It happens on 5th November, just like everywhere else in the country. But instead of burning a Guy, Liverpudlians burn an effigy of Boris Johnson. You'll often hear Scouse kids going door-to-door shouting 'Penny for the Boris?'

> *"Who can forget the fab four, those cheeky moptops **The Kinks?**"*

LOCAL TRIVIA

• The song 'You'll Never Walk Alone' was originally written by a surgeon about a pair of Siamese twins.

• Liverpool's most famous musical sons, Half Man Half Biscuit, are actually not from Liverpool, but Birkenhead.

• The stereotype of Scousers with perms, moustaches, shell suits and going on strike is a complete fiction. There have been no strikes in Liverpool this week.

SCOUSE-O-METER

1 **Cilla** *'lorra lorra love'* **Black**
2 **Jimmy** *'oh ohhh'* **Tarbuck**
3 **Derek** *'can you feel that'* **Acorah**
4 **Ken** *'how much tax!'* **Dodd**
5 **Kim** *'?'* **Cattrall**

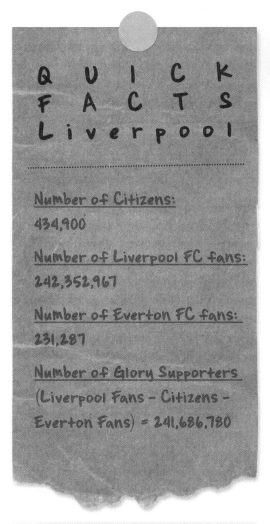

QUICK FACTS Liverpool

Number of Citizens:
434,900

Number of Liverpool FC fans:
242,352,967

Number of Everton FC fans:
231,287

Number of Glory Supporters
(Liverpool Fans - Citizens -
Everton Fans) = 241,686,780

NEWCASTLE

HISTORY

The Vikings founded Newcastle and their descendants are the race that we now call Geordies. Them's not my words, them's the words of the great Charles Darwin, who was the first man to discover this link:

> 'During my extensive studies I noticed that Geordies never wore coats. And then it struck me; have you ever seen Vikings wearing coats? No? Exactly! So Geordies must be descended from Vikings. And with that categorical proof, I wrapped up my studies early and had a few Brown Ales down the Quayside.'
>
> Charles Darwin, On the Origin of Species

The name 'Newcastle' derives from the fact that a new castle is built in the city every single year. During Thatcher's reign, government cutbacks meant that no new castles were built between the years 1984 and 1988. During this time, the city was known as Oldcastle.

*"Do not be alarmed if any of your fellow passengers are engaging in **love-making activities...**"*

NORTH

SCOTLAND

Newcastle

WALES

OTHER LESS IMPORTANT PLACES (IE. THE SOUTH)

TRAVEL

Newcastle has a wonderful mechanical tram service known as the Metro. The city planners are hopeful that within the next fifty years the tramlines will be upgraded to tarmac roads, wide enough for motorcars to travel on.

When travelling on the tram system, do not be alarmed if any of your fellow passengers are engaging in love-making activities. This activity is commonplace on public transport in Newcastle and is called 'Metro-sexual intercourse'.

NIGHTLIFE

Newcastle is renowned for its exciting nightlife. If drinking, fighting and wearing next to nothing is your bag, then it's well worth a go. Top nightspots include:

• **BIGG MARKET** Under new EU directives drawn up for this stretch of pubs and clubs, British law doesn't count. Anything goes. Rumours of Bigg Market changing its name to the Kerry Katona Mile are totally unfounded.

• **THE CLUB THAT'S ON THE PADDLE BOAT** I'm not entirely sure what this club is actually called. It seems to change its name more often than Puff Daddy – but I can tell you that it's a lot of fun. Plus, it has a revolving dance floor. Or maybe I was just hammered when I went there. Or maybe even both. Nevertheless, a smashing night out.

• **QUAYSIDE** This is the cosmopolitan area of Newcastle – people from all over the world come to drink in the swish bars. People from places like

*"Drinking, fighting and **wearing next to nothing...**"*

Argentina, Brazil, Peru... basically, whichever countries Newcastle United are currently signing players from. Don't worry too much about this language barrier, the Geordie accent can easily be picked up, once you've downed a few flaming sambucas.

LANDMARKS

• **ANGEL OF THE NORTH** This iconic statue overlooks the A1 and the roads into Newcastle, and cost a million quid to build. A million quid!? For that? Somebody's in for the high jump at the planning offices. OK, so I'm no art critic, but even I can see its major design flaw. It's only been up ten years and it's already gone rusty – should have spent some of ⟫→

them million pounds on Hammerite – and while we're on the subject, arms don't look like that. Those look like bloody aeroplane wings! Luckily the residents of Newcastle are a forgiving sort and happily go about their day-to-day duties safe in the knowledge that an upside-down rusty aeroplane is watching over them.

• **THE METROCENTRE** Officially Europe's biggest shopping precinct. To give you a feeling of how big this place is, it's got *two* Greggs. *Two* Greggs! Heaven on Earth. It's bold consumer decisions like this that really put Newcastle at the top of the world's best shopping destinations. There are enough Primarks, restaurants and fairground rides in the MetroCentre that you could quite easily live in there for a fortnight. I know that for a fact because I once did. Went for a day's shopping, couldn't find my car afterwards, and ended up turning it into a holiday... TWO GREGGS!!!!!

• **BYKER GROVE** Byker Grove Youth Club – Geordie version of Cambridge University. Past members have gone on to great successes and include the popular singers PJ & Duncan who, after puberty, became the much-loved TV-presenting duo Ant & Dec, the founders of the Gallowgate TV production company and 55% shareholders in the cheeky smile franchise.

PUBLIC HOLIDAYS

• **FESTIVAL OF SHEARER** A seven-week-long festival during which everyone is very enthusiastic at the start but depressed and disillusioned by the end.

• THE DAY OF COATLESS DRINKING

The citizens of Newcastle take to the city centre, not wearing coats, for some drinking shenanigans. This occurs on every Friday and Saturday. And Sunday. And Monday, Tuesday, Wednesday and Thursday. Running indefinitely for ever!

• **FESTIVAL OF KEEGAN** Has some similarities to the 'Festival of Shearer'. Every sixteen years, joyous celebrations fill the streets of Newcastle, during which the local people become illogically optimistic. The next 'Festival of Keegan' is due in 2024.

LOCAL TRIVIA

• It is physically and biologically impossible for Geordies and Mackems (residents of Sunderland) to have sexual intercourse.

• To save money on price tags, the stripes on the Newcastle United shirt double up as a working barcode.

• Notorious Geordie, Jimmy 'Five Bellies', only has one actual belly.

• Reggae music was invented in Newcastle during the late seventies by Sting.

• Tim Healy is the most Geordie Geordie.

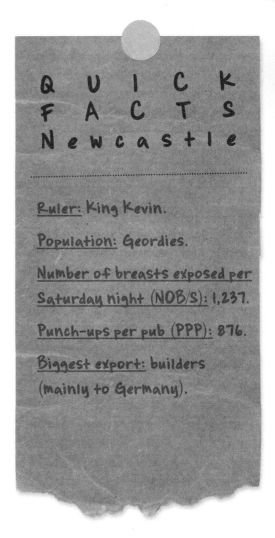

QUICK FACTS Newcastle

Ruler: King Kevin.

Population: Geordies.

Number of breasts exposed per Saturday night (NOB/S): 1,237.

Punch-ups per pub (PPP): 876.

Biggest export: builders (mainly to Germany).

LEEDS

HISTORY

Leeds was granted its Borough charter in 1207 and in the Middle Ages it became a thriving market town. In 1527, Leeds became the first Northern settlement outside of London to have a Harvey Nichols. Though back then, Harvey Nichols just sold designer pigs' trotters and haute couture French gruel.

In more recent times, Leeds played a notable role in the Industrial Revolution and its citizens were a key inspiration to Britain during the Second World War, as referenced in Winston Churchill's famous speech:

'We shall defend our island, whatever the cost may be. We shall fight them on the beaches, we shall fight on the landing grounds. And if Adolf doesn't call it a day there, we shall fight them on the terraces and I'll send some of them Leeds boys in. Then those Nazi bastards will be sorry.'

Winston Churchill, 1940

These days, Leeds City Council is aiming to make the city the 'Capital of the North'. Good luck with that – I don't see Bolton getting knocked off the number one spot any time soon.

ATTRACTIONS

• ROYAL ARMOURIES MUSEUM
This building contains some excellent and informative displays dedicated to war, arms, hunting and military horsemanship. The museum brings to life warfare conditions from medieval times all the way through to the present day, including Asian weaponry and live jousting battles.

> *"They serve up some great food and if you get a bit sleepy,* **no one minds you having a doze.**"

However, those visitors hoping to find live re-enactments of Elland Road hooligan battles from the 1980s or of the riotous Leeds Festival rampage of 2002 will be sadly disappointed (those shows don't open until 2014).

• THE LEEDS/READING FESTIVAL
I haven't actually been to this, but anything that encourages young people to do more reading can only be a good thing. It's great that so many cool pop stars go along to this reading festival too. I can't think of anything that would make me want to read books more than Rage Against the Machine reading extracts of *The Da Vinci Code,* or the *Arctic Monkeys* doing passages from *Harry Potter and the Deathly Hallows.* I might go there myself one day – that is, if I ever read a book. Truth be told, I haven't even read this one all the way through and I wrote the bastard.

• HEADINGLEY CRICKET GROUND
I'll tell you what, I can guarantee a cracking time if you try 'heading' along here with a few pals. They've got a great selection of lagers and bitters, a wonderful atmosphere, and some of the loveliest and friendliest people you'll ever meet – it's hours of fun. They serve up some great food and if you get a bit sleepy, no one minds you having a doze. It really is the perfect day out. Someone once told me that there are some fellas playing a game on that grassy bit in the middle, but I can't say I've ever noticed it myself. Too busy with the drink and chatting. ≫→

MUSIC

Leeds has produced its fair share of musical talent over the years. Here's my pick of the bunch:

> "The Kaiser Chiefs are fronted by the brilliant One Foot in the Grave actor, **Richard (Ricky) Wilson.**"

comedy work to pursue a career in the indie music scene. When it came to song-writing, Ricky drew from his own experiences when he used Victor Meldrew's well-known catchphrase to earn the band their biggest hit, 'Oh My God – I Don't Believe It!' Some have accused the Kaiser Chiefs of sounding a bit like Blur. I don't agree with that. For starters, they don't have Northern accents... Actually, that's also for finishers as well.

• **THE SPICE GIRLS (ONE-FIFTH OF THEM, ANYWAY – MEL B)** Regardless of which Spice Girls track you listen to, it's hard to miss those unmistakable West Yorkshire influences throughout (one-fifth of) every single one of their songs. Without Leeds, the world would never have had (one-fifth of) The Spice Girls, (one-fifth of) the film Spice World, or (half of) the hit song 'I Want You Back' by Melanie B (featuring Missy 'Misdemeanor' Elliott). Ultimately, when history looks back on the 20th century, our descendants will realise that, without Leeds, (one-fifth of) 'Girl Power' would never exist.

• **KAISER CHIEFS** The Kaiser Chiefs are fronted by the brilliant One Foot in the Grave actor, Richard (Ricky) Wilson. In 2000, Richard gave up his successful

• **CHRIS MOYLES** The 'saviour of Radio 1' is Leeds born and bred and, when it comes to disc jockeys, this fella is top of his game. Few Radio 1 breakfast DJs have been more likeable than Mr Moyles – except, perhaps (and off the top of my head), Tony Blackburn, Noel Edmonds, Dave Lee Travis, Mike Read, Mike Smith, Simon Mayo, Mark

Goodier, Steve Wright, Chris Evans, Mark & Lard, Kevin Greening and Zoe Ball, Sara Cox, Tim Westwood, etc., etc., etc.

PUBLIC HOLIDAYS

• **LEEDS LIGHTS** Every Christmas, the people of Leeds descend on Victoria Gardens for the turning on of the Christmas lights. Over the years, the lights have been turned on by such names as Chico, Leon Jackson and Same Difference. Some years they even get celebrities to do it.

• **REMEMBRANCE DAY** This is a fortnightly event which happens in the Elland Road area every other Saturday. At about 3 p.m., in a completely uncoordinated event, thousands of Loiners turn to each other and say 'Remember when we used to be in the top flight?'

LOCAL TRIVIA

• Leeds earned the nickname 'Dirty Leeds' because its citizens have the fewest baths per household in Britain.

• The biggest thing to come out of Leeds is Chris Moyles.

• In the eighties, during the height of football violence, Leeds was twinned with South Central LA, Beirut and Mogadishu.

• No one in Leeds owns their own car. They own someone else's.

QUICK FACTS Leeds

Most popular man in Leeds (1997–2001): Peter Ridsdale.

Most popular phrase in Harvey Nichols, Leeds:
'*How* much for a pair of socks!'

Official Leeds City anthem:
'I Predict a Riot' by the Kaiser Chiefs.

Least popular man in Leeds (2001–present): Peter Ridsdale.

Join the dots

PUZZLE 1

CLUE: A popular pastime for London men...

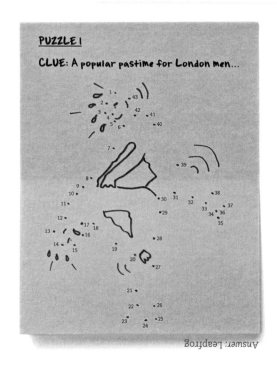

PUZZLE 2

CLUE: Costume sometimes worn by citizens of Oldham when attending secret get-togethers...

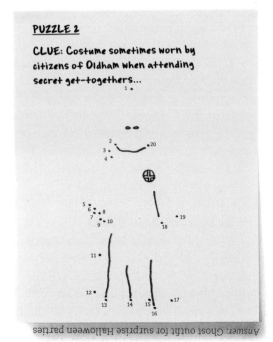

PUZZLE 3

CLUE: The number one way for youths to make money in Southern inner cities...

PUZZLE 4

CLUE: A very profitable business on Merseyside...

32

!CAUTION!

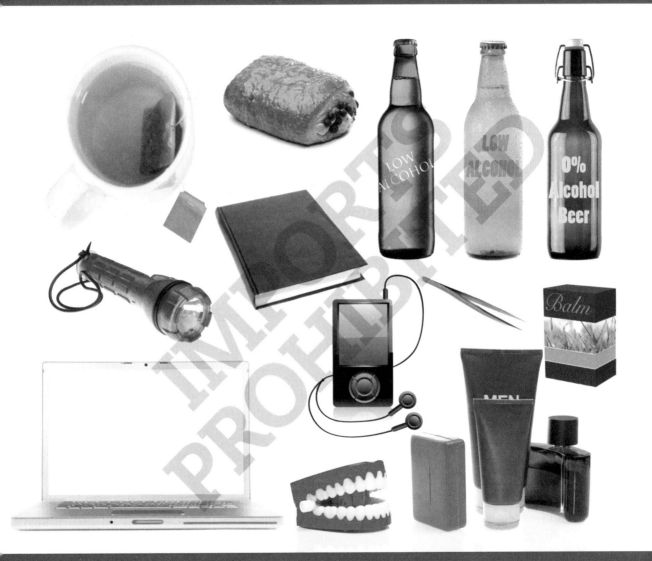

NORTHERN BORDER AUTHORITIES

If you are travelling from the south into the North, in the interests of retaining our Northernness you are not permitted to bring the following items into our region »

CONTINENTAL PASTRIES

All croissants/pains au chocolate and Viennese whirls will be exchanged for sausage rolls and custard creams.

MALE GROOMING PRODUCTS

Other than coal tar soap, supermarket own-brand mouthwash and Tabac aftershave.

ELECTRONIC EQUIPMENT

All magic-light wizardry that might scare or dazzle Northerners will be confiscated at Border Control and incinerated.

NON-ALCOHOLIC BEER

Only beers over 10% alcohol may be carried into the North. Certain alco-pops may need a licence.

SELF-HELP BOOKS

Border Control guards will seize any such literature and give the owner a little but beneficial slap.

HERBAL TEAS

Builders' tea only may pass through Border Control. None of that perfumed shite.

TWEEZERS

Male travellers are not permitted to carry these items as there is no conceivable need they could have for a pair.

HUMOUR

Southern travellers will be asked to tell three jokes, of which one must at least raise a wry smile. Faces like smacked arses must be left in London.

HISTORY OF
THE NORTH

⚑ 4 BC

Birth of Christ in Bolton. On the site of the very stable in which Mary and Joseph slept that fateful night, there's now a Lidl. They have not forgotten the place's heritage though, as they only open for half a day on Sundays, which I presume is some sort of tribute.

500 BC | **0 BC** | **50 AD** | **100 AD** | **200 AD**

⚑ 79 AD

Mr Agricola, a Roman, comes to visit (marches in with armies) and stays (occupies) for a bit (330 years).

⚑ 133 AD

Bolton Wanderers FC wins the World Cup. Unfortunately, pens, football pitches, grass or the game of football weren't yet invented – hence no one has a clue about it.

⚑ 978 AD

Aethelred the Unready, in his first act as the new king of England, commissions the first series of long-running Northern-based BBC 1 sitcom *Last of the Summer Wine*.

⚑ 500 AD

Some friendly German-speaking folk called the Angles come and stay for a while. They might have had a funny name, but anyone who laughed at them was killed – along with anyone who didn't laugh at them as well.

| 250 AD | 500 AD | 750 AD | 1000 AD | 1250 AD |

⚑ 1070 AD

We Northerners invite Frenchman William the Conqueror up for a bit of good-natured conquering. He kills a few of us, we say go away, he kills a few more, we say stop, he initiates a famine. A little bit cold of him.

⚑ 793 AD

The Vikings pop over for the first time from Denmark to see what the North is like. Problem for the locals was, they quite liked it. Who can blame them? But then they made a habit of popping over uninvited like annoying neighbours. Annoying neighbours with axes and a fondness for pillaging who keep on coming back for seventy-five years until a French bloke called William got involved and told them to stop it.

1455

The start of the Wars of the Roses. The biggest fight the world has ever known over confectionery started in Lancaster. See my Guide to Lancaster on page 158 for more info on this weird period in history.
I prefer the ones in the purple wrappers.

1476

William Caxton, probably a Northerner, fires up the first printing press in England. He rattled off a few copies of *The Canterbury Tales* but then got bored and starting turning out mucky stuff instead. Dave The Oracle still has an early edition of *Ye Reader's Wyfes* from about that time.

1707

Scotland and England join together to form Great Britain. Scotland immediately regretted the decision and tried to rub out its signature from the document, but got told off and had to sit in the corner.

1400 AD 1500 AD 1600 AD 1650 AD 1700 AD

1666

The disastrous Great Fire of London – only mentioned here because it was all down to an irate baker from Wigan. But he wasn't baking at the time, he was actually trying to make some toast using a faulty trouser-press in Savile Row. That's how Dave The Oracle says the whole thing started, anyway.

1688

The Dutch invade. Has everybody quite finished? Anyone else want a go? Is there anyone left who hasn't invaded the North yet?

1926

Scotsman John Logie Baird gives the first working demonstration of telly. The first images seen were of Compo being hit round the head by Nora Batty in the long-running BBC 1 sitcom *Last of the Summer Wine*.

1926

More importantly this year, the Trotters do it again! 1-0 in the FA Cup final at Wembley against Man City thanks to a seventy-sixth-minute scorcher from David Jack. Old Grandad McGuinness said, scrap the other one, in fact this was the best day of his life – because he was touting tickets outside the ground at a 500% mark-up.

1923

The Wanderers win the FA Cup by beating West Ham FC. Old Grandad McGuinness said it was the best day of his life because while everyone was out watching the match, he went round to their houses to pinch their stuff.

  1750 AD 1800 AD 1850 AD 1900 AD 1950 AD

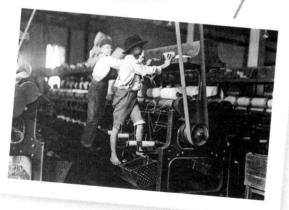

1929

Another FA Cup! Three times in six years! Portsmouth didn't get a look-in and it ended 2-0. Old Grandad McGuinness said it was the best day of his life. He was such a liar when it came to picking his favourite days.

1833

A new Act comes into force which means women and children can't work silly hours in the Northern mills. Unfortunately, someone forgot about the blokes so they just had to work even harder to take up the slack.

1958

Britain's first motorway, the M6 Preston Bypass, opens. Why they didn't start at the M1 is anyone's guess and it must have been useless anyway because there weren't any other roads in the North.

1966

England wins the World Cup – thanks mostly to a Northerner, Geoff Hurst.

| 1950 AD | 1955 AD | 1960 AD | 1965 AD | 1970 AD |

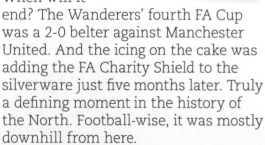

1958

Forget motorways though, it's FA Cup winning time again. When will it end? The Wanderers' fourth FA Cup was a 2-0 belter against Manchester United. And the icing on the cake was adding the FA Charity Shield to the silverware just five months later. Truly a defining moment in the history of the North. Football-wise, it was mostly downhill from here.

1971

'Wild Life', the first album by Wings, is released and reaches number four in the Norwegian album chart. These days of course, you can't think of Liverpool without thinking of Wings and how they went on to become one of the biggest bands in the world.

1973

Paddy McGuinness is born.

1998

The Angel of the North lands in Gateshead. Nobody knows where it came from, what it's doing there, or when it'll take off again. One of the North's great unsolved mysteries...

 1975 AD   1980 AD   1990 AD   2000 AD   2020 AD

2010

Paddy McGuinness writes a book. It's an amazing book and everyone in England buys a copy. They invent a new award at the Oscars just for books and give it to Paddy, to no one's surprise and everyone's delight, especially other comedians.

1975

Ant & Dec are born. And so it begins.

SOUTHERN LANDMARKS

REMODELLED

Whatever you think of the Angel of the North (and you probably think that it's a waste of good iron), the south of England does seem to have more than its fair share of landmarks – Wembley Stadium, Cheddar Gorge, Canterbury Cathedral, Warwick Castle, the Houses of Parliament, the Queen... What have us Northerners got to look at? If you discount bridges, nuclear power stations and bloody great rusty angels, then the answer's not a lot.

But that's not to say those southern landmarks can't be improved. Oh no. And I know just the man to do it: me. What I propose is that we build improved versions of the best two or three southern landmarks up here in the North. I'm no engineer, architect or accountant, but I reckon I know enough about engineering, architecture and accountiture to make it happen. Here are my (admittedly rough) blueprints.

1 › THE NEW WEMBLEY

STADIUM 2

The new Wembley Stadium looks very nice and all, but why oh why did they build it in London? That's in the south. Not the North. And I'll be buggered if I'm going down there (well, that's according to Dave The Oracle anyhow). I say we build a bigger, better New Wembley Stadium 2 somewhere closer to Bolton – say... in Bolton. And this is what it will look like...

- For a start, it should have two towers.

- The pitch/screen is obviously open air, we don't want to feel claustrophobic.

- To be one better than the old New Wembley, the New Wembley Stadium 2 will have seats AND, this will blow your socks off, STANDING as well. We must have access to the bar.

- The whole thing will be heated by one massive radiator that goes all the way around the outside. It can get nippy around the -10 mark.

- No need for a car park, we'll all be walking from the pub – well, it is the pub.

- I, as the designer, will have my own leather swivel seat as near to the screen as is safe, without causing an epileptic fit.

- Undoubtedly, with a stadium of this quality, some southerners will want to come and frequent it. For that reason, there will be a few portable 10in TVs dotted around the outside. These will be accompanied by booths selling warm cans of beer at twelve times the normal RRP.

Total project cost (estimate):

£2,500 – £3,000

2 › PVC HENGE
CONSERVATORY

OK, so it might have been built by wizards in the time of the dinosaurs, but that's no excuse for letting it fall to bits. Only half of the stones are left nowadays apparently – and the ones that are there are all different shapes and sizes and scratched.

The whole thing needs dragging into the 20th century – which is where I can help.

For a start, it's far too stony. Let's make it half the size and build it entirely out of PVC – good, solid PVC what that Cannon & Ball are flogging at the minute. Also, make it square because circles are really hard to draw and, according to Bobby Ball, the moulding machine is already set to squares.

Plus – and I can't believe the wizards didn't think of this – the thing needs a roof. A bit of transparent corrugated plastic would keep the rain out while also letting people see the sun (more

likely to be cloud), the moon (cloud again), or whatever else it is people want to see from in there.

The crowds that come visiting will probably want some form of refreshment, so one corner of PVC Henge Conservatory could double as a bar. And maybe put a pie oven in there too.

Hey presto! The world's biggest conservatory/celestial star map would piss all over that dated stone debacle. Now, which Northern town wants it? I was thinking it could go in Bolton, just down the road from the New Wembley Stadium 2.

PVC

Total project cost:

£950 (estimate based on a similar job which Tommy Cannon had done on his front porch)

3 › NORTHERN EYE

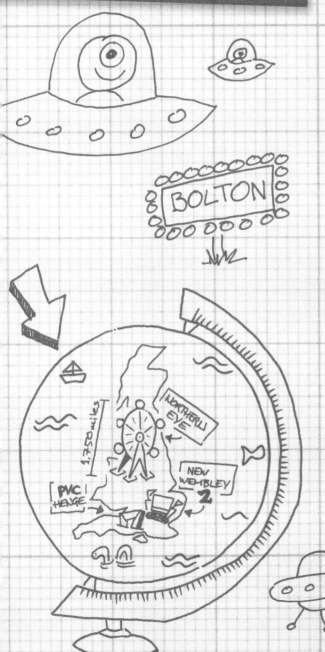

BOLTON

1,750 miles

PVC HENGE

NORTHERN EYE

NEW WEMBLEY 2

Londoners are always bleating on about the London Eye which, when all's said and done, is really just a big Ferris wheel painted white with big plastic eggs glued over the seats. Blackpool already has a perfectly good wheel on the Central Pier so we don't really need another one, but in the interests of levelling the North–south landmark deficit, I believe we should have the following:

What the North needs is a Ferris wheel visible from space. The Great Wall of China is visible from space and that's 5,500 miles long. So, by my maths, the Northern Eye will need to be 1,750 miles tall to compete. That's taller than the Beetham Tower in Manchester, which I know is hard to believe. So here's a scale drawing to help...

Sounds expensive – and it is – plus, I'd probably need to go on a evening course to get a BTEC or two before building something like this. But here's the clever part: a wheel that big could fit everyone from London on it at the same time – with enough seats left over for Sheffield. Then, it could accidentally break down for a bit, making the rest of the UK very happy. I'd be a hero and people would flock to Bolton! Because that's where we should have it – in between PVC Henge and the New Wembley Stadium 2.

Total project cost (estimate):

where do I start?

WHAT MEN REALLY WANT

Us men are simple beasts. For example, I may want to attract the attention of a lovely lady... I just send my mate over to ask you out. Easy.

Having spoken to many a man, I have compiled the definitive list of what is going on inside a bloke's head.

WHAT NORTHERN MEN REALLY WANT

Simple. We want our females to look good but not take too long doing it. It should take, what, three minutes to shower? Another two minutes to throw on an outfit? And nought minutes to do your make-up (you can do that on the bus). I can't see any reason for it to take longer than five minutes. Here's a suggestion: Why not get up to speed with regular time trials? You could even invite a friend over as a pacemaker. You'll be down to 2 mins 30 secs in no time.

If you take time getting changed, then you have to accept that us blokes will make our own entertainment – which comes at a cost. Please understand that you can't just 'pause' a game of Modern Warfare II. There are objectives to be obtained – you can't just go saving games willy-nilly. Allow at least 30 minutes to an hour for this.

A pint! Simple as that, a nice pint of the old gold and cold to wash away the day's misery and the thoughts of what could have been had we made the right career decisions.

Five minutes on our own. Just five minutes when we walk through the door – that's not too much to ask, is it?

Now. If you want to know the really inner workings of a Northern man's mind then read the next bit very carefully as I'm going to let you in to a secret. Men think about 'How's your father' quite a lot. But don't believe everything you read; we don't think about it every seven seconds. No. Us blokes can go for up to ninety minutes without thinking about sex. Even longer if there's injury time.

WHAT SOUTHERN (LONDON) MEN REALLY WANT

Face creams.

Hampstead Heath.

The Pet Shop Boys.

Football, especially that Ronaldo.

Rugby, especially that Jonny Wilkinson.

Vegetarianism.

Answers to string theory.

Keep in mind that, like their Northern counterparts, men from the south (London) don't think about sex every seven seconds either – well at least not with women. They think about the Large Hadron Collider every seven seconds. They may be considering how to improve it, will it offend people of other cultures, or find the information it produces slightly arousing.

The southern (London) man doesn't want a woman with a sense of humour, he doesn't want a woman with a good career, he doesn't want a woman with principles, a woman with a nice figure, a woman with strong opinions, a woman who could suck a golf ball through a hose pipe. Let's face it, he doesn't want a WOMAN.

What Women Really Want

What do women really want? I'll be honest. I haven't got a scooby. Looking into a woman's mind is like looking into an IT department. It's a mess, and if you press the wrong buttons you get shouted at. So I've had to do a bit of research on this one. Yesterday I popped down the library to find out more – but it was shut. So I did a bit more research and found that the library isn't open on a Sunday. Then I got into the library and had to do some research on how to use a cataloguing system. So I basically gave up, came home, put on the kettle, and just wrote down whatever came to mind.

What Northern Women Really Want

They want a man who can make them laugh. To be clear, I'm not talking about laughing 'with' you, I'm talking about laughing 'at' you. You know... if you hurt yourself, get a fact wrong, or wear clothes that you think look cool. In this situation NEVER try to rationalise what you did, 'cos that's a war you can never win, my son. All you can do is bottle up your frustration

and, perhaps ten years down the line, it'll all finally get on top of you and you can erupt in an explosion of screaming anger. When this happens, your partner will, no doubt, laugh at you.

*"It's important to realise that what applies to her **doesn't apply to you...**"*

'Do you like this dress?' she asks. Of course the correct answer is NO! But in this situation, honesty is definitely NOT the best policy.

It's not about 'correct' answers, is it? This is one of the many situations where it's OK to lie. (It's also OK to lie when asked 'Do you think Debs from work is attractive?', 'Where have you been?' and 'Were you the last one to use my computer?') It's important to realise that what applies to her doesn't apply to you… so whatever you do, do not laugh at her dress. When confronted with this question, you need to say 'It looks good', but you MUST say it within a quarter of a second or else she will know something's up. Try practising this with your mate down the pub, because you need to be faster than Usain Bolt out of the starting blocks.

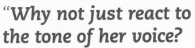

> ## "Why not just react to the tone of her voice?
> *If she sounds happy and pleased you say, 'That's great. Well done, love'"*

A female friend of mine once told me that women like a man who listens (at least I think that's what she said – *Top Gear* was on so I wasn't really paying attention). You have two options here: you can try and genuinely listen to what she has to say. But that can be too much like hard work. So instead why not just react to the tone of her voice? If she sounds happy and pleased you say, 'That's great. Well done, love', and if she sounds angry say, 'Tut. That's terrible…' Job done! Don't worry if you don't hear her mention important information like dates, names or something you needed to do – that's why God invented nagging. Didn't hear what she said? You'll definitely have another opportunity or five to hear it again.

What Southern Women Really Want

I find reading southern women as easy as reading Stephen Hawking's *A Brief History of Time*. I'm saying both are very difficult, Einstein. And I find listening to southern women as easy as listening to the audiobook of *A Brief History of Time* read by Stephen Hawking. Again, both difficult. Nevertheless, here are a few tips and tricks for understanding the non-Northern lady.

If she talks to you she's definitely interested – the girls down there don't talk to just anyone – in fact they just don't talk to anyone. Now – there is one exception to this rule. If the conversation starts with 'No, I don't have any spare change'. In that situation, chances of pulling are nil.

You can't just buy her half a mild and expect her to be yours for the rest of the evening, oh no. The southern ladies only react to posh drinks like Port and Malibu... basically, if you can

> *"The southern ladies only react to posh drinks like* **Port and Malibu...***"*

imagine James Bond or Sherlock Holmes drinking it, it's OK. So that rules out WKD, Ouzo and Lambrini.

The hardest part is conversation. You need to appear like you're worldly wise. If you're feeling minted, then why not invest in a newspaper from that day, memorise some of the opinions, and repeat them back parrot fashion to her. If you can't afford such riches, try getting her talking with one of the following phrases:

'I can't believe what the Prime Minister of our country has been up to. What do you think about that?'

> "If all else fails, **tell them you're big mates** with needs-a-good-wash-comedian, **Russell Brand.**"

'I was looking at some science the other day and I discovered an entirely new thing... but enough about me. Have you discovered any good science recently?'

'So I was thinking about history the other day. I probably love the 1200s the most for lots of reasons I won't go into here, but what's YOUR favourite bit of history?'

'Yesterday I went into the London art gallery and I'll tell you what, I loved that art in there. Many people say that the art there looks like a big pile of shit that any six-year-old could make, but I think it's cleverer than that because it's art, isn't it? What do you think about art?'

And if she's not putty in your arms after smooth talk like that, then she's probably a lesbian. Which a lot of them are down there because it's fashionable to be one, so don't be surprised.

If all else fails, tell them you're big mates with needs-a-good-wash-comedian, Russell Brand. He's slept with them all!

Paddy's VOUCHERS

I've got a big heart. And you know what they say about people with big hearts – grossly overweight or genetic freaks. However, I'm neither – I'm just kind. And to prove it, here's a wealth of money-saving vouchers for you to cut out and keep*. They're accepted all across the North of England** and to get hold of these discounts for you, I've personally done deals with all my favourite places – so get ready for some good old family fun!***

*By which I mean 'tear out and use'

**Within a three-mile radius of Bolton

***Some attractions aren't really suitable for children

SAMI'S KEBABS
FARNWORTH

Buy any large kebab or chicken burger meal after 1 a.m. on a Saturday night and present this voucher to get a free fight

(normal RRP £3.99).

Pie
Meat pies 80p
Just about anywhere.

BOLTON BETAMAX RENTALS

This voucher entitles the bearer to a lifetime membership of Bolton Betamax Rentals. That means you can visit the shop as often as you like – and, what's more, your first rental is absolutely free! Like action films? We've got *Under Siege* – just in! Like romance? Why not try the brand-new erotic thriller *Indecent Proposal*. Like adventure? You'll be wowed by *Waterworld*. Like some other sort of movies? Tricky – we've only got those three. But we plan to buy a fourth film if business goes well in the next few months.

TERMS & CONDITIONS: Fourth film may not be coming soon. Lifetime membership confers no quantifiable benefits. First come, first served – we've only got one copy of each tape and even then the *Waterworld* one is cracked.

ROXY'S NIGHTCLUB

CARLISLE: FREE COAT OR JACKET

Cut out this voucher and present it to the cloakroom staff at Roxy's, preferably after about 11.30 p.m. when everyone's in. Then we will give you a free coat or jacket. Might be a man's, might be a lady's – who knows? So come and party with us at Roxy's!

'Roxy's – who knows what you'll end up with, but it'll be better than nothing'

FREE FABERGÉ EGG

Just collect twenty wrappers from promotional packs of **Opal Fruits** or **Marathon bars**, plus ten ring-pulls from **Tab Clear** or **Quatro** and **400 Esso Tiger Tokens**. Then redeem them at your local **Woolworth's** or **C&A** store.

Obtaining your own priceless artefact for free really is that easy.

Mindy's MASSAGE PARLOUR

Present this voucher when you purchase one 'Finesse' massage and receive a 'Finesse Xxxtra' bolt-on mini-massage immediately after your main treatment. Please, no women, children, police officers or men with pacemakers.

MERSEYSIDE MANOR PARK & ZOO

Come and experience a day out to remember at Merseyside's newest attraction! There's not a great deal to do yet as it isn't quite finished. But come and see the amazing sight of where the zoo will go! And witness the wonder of where the park will be! At the very least, a couple of the roads are finished and they've got two foxes who sometimes go through the bins so it's well worth a visit.

Special Offer: present this voucher at the Portakabin at the entrance and receive a free hour's use of a spade!

Missed × Connections

 Women Seeking Men:

> **NORTH »** You – man in Revolution vodka bar with white shirt and spiky hair. Me – lass who showed you her right tit in the disabled toilets. Wanna see the left one?

> **SOUTH •** You – Lord Penbury of Buckinghamshire eating stuffed swan at the pleasure of Lord and Lady Farquhar in Hampton Court Palace. Me – lady waltzing with the Duke of Ponsonbury. More swan?

Finding true love can be hard. All of us spend our lives looking for 'the one' (although my mate Baz managed to find himself 'the three'... but he's hoping they'll never meet). We all want to find Miss Right (or, in Baz's case, Mrs Right... but he's hoping Mr Right never finds out).

You might spot your perfect partner on the bus, in a shop or through the bushes – but how do you let them know how you feel? How can you contact that special person when you've never even spoken to them? The answer is you put a Missed Connections ad in the local paper. It's a bit like stalking, but more romantic.

Here are a few cuttings from Britain's local papers that show the different kinds of courtship found up and down the country.

> **SOUTH »** Norwich Barn Dance, last Saturday. You – my cousin. Me – your sister. Coffee?

> **NORTH •** You – kicking four colours of shit out of that Billy Eccleston outside a closed-down pet shop. Me – in boob tube shouting 'Smash his cheating face in!' Bacardi Breezer?

♥ Men Seeking Women:

SOUTH • You – attempting to sabotage a hunt in the grounds of my estate. Me – shooting at all the crusties from my Bentley. High tea?

SOUTH » You – magical nanny dancing on rooftop with some blacked-up men. Me – Cockney/Australian/South African chimney sweep. Fancy a spoonful of sugar?

NORTH » You – girl having a slanging match with your boyfriend on Clitheroe bus station. Me – female bus driver of the 482. Wondering if you fancy a change from those bastard men?

NORTH • You – hairy lady looking for ciggies in a bin. Me – man vomiting into a Maccy D's paper cup. Dinner?

♥ Men Seeking Men:

SOUTH » You – gorgeous cashmere thin-knit and leather clutch-bag getting your hair styled in the seat nearest the window last Tuesday. Me – styling your hair in the seat nearest the window last Tuesday. Cocktail?

NORTH • N/A

"Dictionary & Phrasebook"

People down south speak funny. There, I've said it. But that's the benefit of being Northern, see. You can just say what you mean. Unlike southerners. They speak all sorts of gobble-dee-gook. And if you happen to find yourself down there (God forbid!) you might like a little help with the lingo. Well, allow me...

Conversation & Essentials

Eh-oop
- Good day.

Mornin'
- Good morning.

Nah then
- Now then.

How do?
- Hello there. How are you?

Alreet?
- Hello there. How are you?

Notser bad.
- I'm in good health, thank you for asking.

Ta
- Yes, thank you. Thanks. Thanks a lot. Thank you. Thanks. Bye.

Howay
- Do come along!

Soz
- I'm so utterly incredibly sorry, old chap, I really cannot apologise enough. I've been an absolute terror and I extend my sincerest apologies, my good friend. It shall never, ever happen again.

Cuppa please chuck
- One grande, skinny, half-caff, vanilla, soya latte to have in please and no, I don't want a pastry thank you.

Shopping & Services

Where's the...
- Excuse me, I'm terribly sorry to bother you, but I wonder if you could perhaps point me in the direction of a...

shop
- Post Office.

shop
- corner shop.

shop
- supermarket.

shop
- Ladbrokes.

shop
- newsagent's.

shop
- Cash Converters.

shop
- brothel.

Gi's a...
- I'm interested in purchasing a...

Quid?
- How much is this item please?

Don't take the piss, love
- That's a little more than I was hoping to pay.

Oi! Oi, mate! Oi! Oi, mate! Oi! Oi! Oi, mate! Mate! Mate! Mate! Oi! Oi, mate... yeah, can I have the bill? Thanks. You're a goodun, you.
- The bill please.

Transport

Just down the road
- About a mile.

(Pause) Just down the road
- Several miles away.

Round the corner
- An exact mile.

bus pass
- train ticket.

bus pass
- Oyster card.

bus pass
- travelcard.

witchcraft
- helicopter.

Food

Scouse, ta.
- Do you serve a stew composed of mutton, onions, carrots, water and far too many potatoes?

Where's the scran?
- I'll take the meat pie please. And so will my wife.

tea
- dinner.

dinner
- lunch.

muffin
- barm cake.

stottie
- large barm cake.

nudger
- hotdog bread.

oven bottom
- flat barm cake.

barm
- crusty barm cake.

flour cake
- floury barm cake.

bread rolls
- baps.

baps
- tits.

HOW SOUTHERNERS PICTURE NORTHERNERS

Down south, a few myths have built up about what us Northerners actually look like. Well, it's time to put a few things straight and dismiss some of these ridiculous, inaccurate stereotypes.

This – would you believe it – is how southerners picture us...

WHAT SOUTHERNERS THINK NORTHERNERS LOOK LIKE:

Unhappy face. We don't all work underground in the North, you know!

Gravel (in mouth). They really think we cannot afford ciggies?

Tweed flat cap. Nobody except the cast of Last of the Summer Wine wears one of these.

Tweed/woollen-looking suit. It's the 21st century now – there are other fabrics up here!

Pint of ale. This is a totally unfair portrayal of us.

Whippet. What an outdated stereotype this is.

Of course, us modern-day Northerners don't look like this in the slightest. So southerners, look at the next page to see what we really look like – and prepare to have your minds opened and your preconceptions shattered.

WHAT NORTHERNERS ACTUALLY LOOK LIKE

See! We look much happier in real life! (Underneath that muck and soot, I can assure you there's a beaming smile.)

Felt cap. We can't afford tweed caps up here. Who do you think we are? Phillip Schofield?

Ciggie. In the North, an unfiltered roll-up is the preferred method of getting tobacco into our systems.

Day-to-day, we don't wear tweed suits either. They're only for special occasions – like funerals for colleagues who've died in factory/mine/workhouse accidents.

Just one pint of ale? In your dreams! We always have at least two on the go at any one time.

Maybe we had whippets three or four years back – but these lads ate them all.

Job done! I'm so glad to have put those ridiculous stereotypes to bed once and for all. Let no more be said about the matter.

HOW NORTHERNERS PICTURE SOUTHERNERS

Later in this book I tell of my frustration about southerners having dated stereotypes of what us Northerners look like. But, in the interests of fairness, I must admit that us lot have the odd preconception about southerners too. But I have in fact been down south once or twice and Dave The Oracle has visited on numerous occasions on business. So, based on our collated research, it's time to debunk some more myths and bring the country that little bit closer together.

WHAT NORTHERNERS THINK SOUTHERNERS LOOK LIKE:

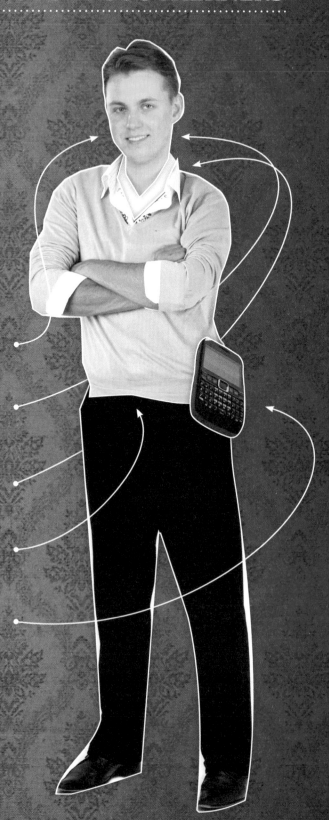

Smug look. Sure, some of the bankers down there look smug, but they're not all bankers.

Bright white teeth. Such unrealistic whiteness! You might be surprised, but some southerners use NHS dentists just like we do.

Upturned collar. What a cliché! Not all of them went to Eton, you know! Some went to Harrow and Radley instead.

Pink pullover. Just because they always drink half pints it doesn't mean they all own pink jumpers too.

Mobile phone. They're not on their mobile phones all the time! They do sometimes communicate with each other using 'talking' as well. Though not on public transport.

OK, so maybe there are a handful of southerners who look like this, but the vast majority don't. So, my Northern brothers and sisters, it's time to take the blinkers from your eyes and see what the modern-day southerner is really like...

WHAT SOUTHERNERS ACTUALLY LOOK LIKE

Moustache. These days, southerners have grown moustaches as a way to hide their smug grins.

All southerners are so rich that they only smoke big fat cigars.

Umbrella is just for show as it never rains down south.

This bell is used to summon a butler who then makes a mobile phone call on behalf of the southerner.

Posh shoes. These are never removed. Not even for intercourse.

So, after this exercise I think we've all learned a valuable lesson about pigeonholing and prejudging people. Whether you are a decent, honest, working-class Northern miner or a posh, pretentious, ex-public school southern investment banker, there is no place for stereotyping in today's society. Case closed.

HOLMFIRTH

HISTORY

Little is known about Holmfirth pre-1973. But in that year the BBC started to film the long-running BBC 1 sitcom *Last of the Summer Wine* in and around the town, finally putting Holmfirth on the map. Up until then, nobody had bothered putting it on the map, which had made it very difficult for the BBC film crews to find it. The choice of location was hailed a masterstroke by celluloid legends of the time.

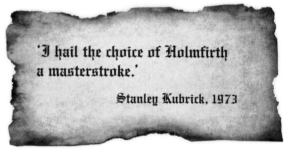

'I hail the choice of Holmfirth a masterstroke.'

Stanley Kubrick, 1973

During the 1980s, Holmfirth was perhaps most famous for being the location of the long-running BBC 1 sitcom *Last of the Summer Wine,* while in the nineties the town gained more of a reputation for being the home of long-running BBC 1 sitcom *Last of the Summer Wine.*

But now, at the dawn of the 21st century, Holmfirth has entered a new era – an era where it has quickly established itself as the town in which the long-running BBC 1 sitcom *Last of the Summer Wine* was filmed, and its first Chinese resident, 'Burt Kwok', star of *Last of the Summer Wine*. But who knows what the 2010s will hold for Holmfirth?

LANDMARKS

• **SID'S CAFÉ** While Sid's Café is perhaps most famous for being a regular location in the long-running BBC 1 sitcom *Last of the Summer Wine,* it also serves food and drink like a normal café. Definitely worth a visit if you're a fan of *Last of the Summer Wine.* Or if you're peckish.

> *"Two Pints of Lager and a Packet of Crisps is not filmed in Holmfirth."*

• **NORA BATTY'S COTTAGE** This self-catering accommodation is located in the house that doubled as Nora Batty's house in the long-running BBC 1 sitcom *Last of the Summer Wine.* You really should visit if you're a fan of *Last of the Summer Wine.*

• **'BATHTUB HILL'** This hill was dubbed 'Bathtub Hill' because it featured in a hilarious incident involving a bath tub and an elderly gentleman which was filmed for a long-running BBC 1 sitcom entitled *Last of the Summer Wine.* ≫→

FAMOUS VISITORS

• **BILL OWEN** Before his sad death in 1999, *Last of the Summer Wine* legend Bill Owen could often be seen playing the part of Compo when the long-running BBC 1 sitcom *Last of the Summer Wine* was filming in Holmfirth.

• **JUNE WHITFIELD** The star of *Terry and June* has been known to work in Holmfirth, predominantly while performing in the long-running BBC 1 sitcom *Last of the Summer Wine.*

• **KANYE WEST** This hip-hop legend was spotted on the Holmfirth 'TV Locations Tour' which takes in the filming locations of a wide array of hit BBC 1 sitcoms, including the long-running *Last of the Summer Wine.*

PUBLIC HOLIDAYS

• **FILMING DAYS** These are special days in the year when the whole town shuts down to gawp at the BBC film crews who are filming long-running BBC 1 sitcom *Last of the Summer Wine.*

"*Hip-hop legend* **Kanye West** *was spotted on the Holmfirth* **'TV Locations Tour'**"

> *"Last of the Summer Wine isn't the only television show to have been filmed in Holmfirth..."*

LOCAL TRIVIA

• *Last of the Summer Wine* is filmed in Holmfirth.

• *Two Pints of Lager and a Packet of Crisps* is not filmed in Holmfirth.

• *Last of the Summer Wine* isn't the only television show to have been filmed in Holmfirth. In 1988, the BBC used the town as a location for a new comedy series called *First of the Summer Wine*.

• The longest-running sitcom on British TV uses Holmfirth as its filming location. The show's name escapes me right now though...

NORTH

SCOTLAND

Bolton

WALES

OTHER LESS
IMPORTANT PLACES
(IE. THE SOUTH)

Bolton

HISTORY

The North-Western town of Bolton has been in existence for over 2,000 years and the first written references to Bolton can be found in the early editions of the Bible:

> 'And lo, Mary and Joseph did travel to their hometown of Bolton upon a tiny donkey. A shining star appeared over the stable in which they dwelt and there the Saviour of mankind was born. God spoke to the people of the world: "Tis only right that Messiah should be born in't my own country, Bolton". And then Joseph declared to Mary: "This gold, frankincense and myrrh are right bonny and all, but I still want that paternity test.'
>
> Lancastrians, Chapter 6, Verses 12-14

It's worth pointing out that some modern versions of the Bible use Bolton's Hebrew name, 'Bethlehem', but after God chose Bolton to be his own country, the town went on to become a key player in the English Civil War and the Industrial Revolution. Then, in 1905, Albert Einstein turned the eyes of the world towards Bolton once more with his groundbreaking 'Theory of Relativity':

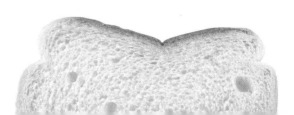

> 'The phenomena of electrodynamics as well as of mechanics possess no properties corresponding to the idea of absolute rest. And, basically, by doing all this maths stuff that I've been doing, I've figured out that Earth doesn't revolve around the poles, as previously thought. No, it actually revolves around a spot located in the centre of a Northern British town called Bolton.'
>
> Albert Einstein, *On the Electrodynamics of Moving Bodies*

These days, Bolton is perhaps most famous for producing some of the greatest British entertainers alive today: Fred Dibnah and, of course... well, you know who I'm going to say, don't you? That's right, an entertainer who's much loved in these parts; someone who might just have written a book which you're reading at the moment. Yes, I'm talking about 'Crush a Grape' legend Stu Francis!

ATTRACTIONS

• **REEBOK STADIUM** Home, of course, to the mighty Bolton Wanderers. Sponsored, of course, by the mighty Bolton-born sportswear manufacturer, Reebok. Now if there's one thing I love more than going to watch the Wanderers, it's going to watch the Wanderers for free. And if there's one thing I love more than wearing quality sportswear, it's wearing quality sportswear that I was given for free. So I'm writing the words 'Bolton Wanderers' and 'Reebok' as many times as I can, in the hope that some of the lovely and highly talented people who work for Bolton Wanderers and Reebok will read this and will, in return for my glowing endorsement and free publicity, send me complimentary tickets and leisure wear.

(Reebok please note: I'm a large for T-shirts/ sweatshirts, a 34-inch waist, 34-inch leg and my shoe size is 9, or 9 and a half, depending on the trainer.)

(Bolton Wanderers FC please note: my eyesight isn't what it was, so I'd probably need seats near the halfway line, about halfway up. Round about where the Premium Executive Boxes are located.)

P.S. Any other sportswear companies, see above. ⋙→

• **BOLTON AQUARIUM** 'Why the hell should I go to Bolton Aquarium?' I hear you say. Well, it might not be the biggest or best aquarium in the world, but Bolton Aquarium does have a unique claim to fame: it's home to the largest known Giant Green Knifefish on the face of the earth. 'Mack', as he is known, moved to the aquarium in 2000 and has attracted thousands of visitors ever since. Also there is an old piranha fish with one eye. So what are you waiting for. Go now!

STOP PRESS: Mack the Giant Green Knifefish died on 16th January 2010 and, come to think of it, so has that bloody piranha!

• **WARBURTONS BAKERY** Warburtons Bakery started in 1876, making bread exclusively for us Boltonians. But since then, the rest of the country has, fortunately for them, discovered Warburtons' excellent baked produce. Town law dictates that, like National Service, everyone in Bolton must do a stint working at Warburtons (I did my bakery conscription back in the nineties). The Warburtons are lovely, but all in bread.

FAMOUS BOLTONIANS

• **SIR IAN McKELLEN** OK, so Macca was actually born in Burnley – he can't help that. But he was educated in Bolton and also started his career in Bolton Theatre, so we can claim him. Like most actors, he didn't get much work for a long time. Then all of a sudden he's the wizard in *Lord of the Rings*, and he's Magneto and in *The Simpsons*. Talk about overnight success!

• **STU FRANCIS** Ooh, he could crush a grape! I know we all could (well, maybe not Stephen Hawking), but the reason I said that is because it was Stu's catchphrase. Stu followed a similar career path to Sir Ian McKellen, except without the boring theatre stuff and knighthood. And instead of being on screen with Tom Hanks, Halle Berry and Nicole Kidman, Stu has been on telly with The Krankies and in panto... erm, with The Krankies!!!

• **FRED DIBNAH** Not only did this man have the best job in the world – climbing up and down things then blowing them up – he was also sponsored by Greenhalghs brewery and drove a steam roller. Every man's dream.

PUBLIC HOLIDAYS

• **REEBOK DAY** Annual day when the generous and gorgeous staff at Reebok send high-quality sportswear to people who have given them some free advertising in any books they might have written.

> "if you say anything bad about Bolton **I'll get Amir Khan to punch your lights out**"

• **SAD DAY** Short for 'Saturday', 'Sad Day' is a weekly event that takes place at around 4.50 p.m. after Bolton Wanderers have played a match. The tradition is that the men of the town act all miserable and sulk for a good few hours while their wives repeat the phrase 'I don't know why he keeps going'.

LOCAL TRIVIA

• The most famous suburb of Bolton is probably Manchester.

• The most picturesque places to visit in Bolton is Queen's Park, Bobby Heywood's Park, Tootles Park and Daubhill.

• Bolton is twinned with other European powerhouses including Madrid, Barcelona, Milan, New York and Munich.

• Not being funny, but if you say anything bad about Bolton I'll get Amir Khan to punch your lights out.

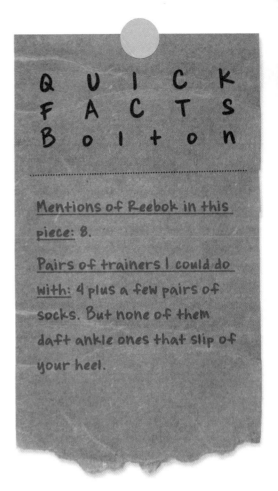

QUICK FACTS Bolton

Mentions of Reebok in this piece: 8.

Pairs of trainers I could do with: 4 plus a few pairs of socks. But none of them daft ankle ones that slip of your heel.

BLACKPOOL

HISTORY

Blackpool's history begins back in Roman times when it was created so that Roman soldiers had somewhere to go on their stag parties. Back then, the illuminations just consisted of a bit of burning hedge and the only ride they had was named 'The Donkey'. Because it was just a donkey. Shakespeare famously documented these events in his play *Julius Caesar*:

NORTH

SCOTLAND

Blackpool

WALES

OTHER LESS
IMPORTANT PLACES
(IE. THE SOUTH)

'Friends, Romans, countrymen, get in the beers! Cos here are the plans for my stag. OK, Gaz – you're on booze duty. Mickey – you're on nicknames so liaise with Tezza, cos he's on T-shirts. Baz – you're driving the stretched chariot. And remember: what happens in Blackpool stays in Blackpool!'

Marcus Antonius in Shakespeare's
Julius Caesar, Act 3, Scene 2

In the 19th century, Blackpool went on to become a popular holiday resort, its piers and Pleasure Beach proving a hit with the tourists. It was during this time that the people of Blackpool invented fancy lights. And to this day, people from all over the North still travel to Blackpool so they can stare in wonder at the illuminations, thinking, 'Wow! Look at that evil electrical witchery. We must burn the people responsible for this.'

These days, Blackpool still brings in millions of visitors every year and the Pleasure Beach remains the most popular tourist attraction in the UK. (Please note: not the 'best', but the 'most popular' – as in *The Jeremy Kyle Show* is very 'popular'.)

"The Pleasure Beach - Forget Disney theme parks, Universal Studios and Alton Towers!"

ATTRACTIONS

• **WINTER GARDENS** Opened in 1878, the twelve venues in the Winter Gardens have played host to The Beatles, Morecambe & Wise, Oasis, George Formby, Mickey Bubbles, Arthur Askey, The Stone Roses, The Labour Party Conference, Lady Gaga, Me and, perhaps most significantly, The World Matchplay Darts Tournament. The Winter Gardens have seen so many legends pass through their doors that it's actually quicker to name the acts that *haven't* played there – the only ones are Chaka Demus & Pliers, Glenn Medeiros and Buju Banton.

• **LOUIS TUSSAUDS** This place is a very popular celebrity hang-out. Last time I went, I bumped into Johnny Depp, Lewis Hamilton, Del Boy, Rodney, and Laurence Llewelyn-Bowen. Be warned though, some of these celebrities can be very cold. I tried to break the ice with Keira Knightley and she just flat-out blanked me for a good twenty minutes. That's celebrities for you though – the fame just makes them all cold and aloof. And, if I'm honest, a little bit waxy.

• **PLEASURE BEACH** Forget Disney theme parks, Universal Studios and Alton Towers! Then, if you have been able to wipe their existence from your brain, Blackpool Pleasure Beach will become the greatest tourist attraction in the world! While thrill-seekers enjoy riding the Grand National, Ice Blast and ≫→

Infusion, I prefer to have a bit of gentle fun on rides like the Monorail and the Tuppenny Machines. Two of the biggest attractions on the Pleasure Beach are the Pepsi Max Big One and the Irn Bru Revolution – so I fully anticipate that next year's new ride will be called the Um Bongo Badboy.

> "Every day the rides on the Pleasure Beach result in the production of **33 litres of vomit.**"

• **DR WHO EXHIBITION** If you like *Doctor Who* and you're in Blackpool, this is a must-see. Don't be put off by the small-looking exterior – it's deceptively big on the inside.

FAMOUS BLACKPUDLIANS

• **SYD LITTLE** The funny-guy partner to Eddie Large's straight man was born and raised in Blackpool. Little and Large got their first big break on *Opportunity Knocks* in 1971 and they

were a mainstay of British TV till 1991 when *The Little & Large Show* ended. I haven't seen them on telly much since, so I can only assume that they're honing Eddie's Benny from *Crossroads* impersonation. One final bit of Syd Little trivia: no one has ever actually seen his eyes.

• **ROBERT SMITH** The lead singer of The Cure was born in Blackpool back in 1959 and, just by looking at him, you can tell he originates from the happiest place on earth. Just thinking of Robert Smith immediately conjures up an image of your typical Blackpudlian – smiley, fun-loving, cheeky and tanned. Sure, The Cure were not as prolific as Black Lace when it came to the hit-making, but he's clearly done well for himself. How else could he afford to dress and look like Russell Brand?

PUBLIC HOLIDAYS

• **EVERY DAY** Every day is a holiday in Blackpool! Every *single* day of the year. It's a year-round party in Blackpool.

> *"Blackpool has the highest number of **lap dancing bars and strip clubs** than anywhere else on the planet."*

The fun doesn't stop whether it's rain or shine. It's just one big old holiday, 24/7, 365 days a year!*

*Holiday season runs April–November.

LOCAL TRIVIA

• Sexual deviants, get those B+Bs booked quick. Blackpool has the highest number of lap dancing bars and strip clubs of anywhere else on the planet… even Amsterdam!

• Piers Morgan's parents loved Blackpool's tourist attractions so much that they named their son after them.

• The Blackpool Tower is much bigger than the Eiffel Tower. (Admittedly, I've never been to Paris to see the Eiffel Tower, but it can't be bigger than the Blackpool Tower, can it? That'd be impossible.)

• If you stacked up all of the donkeys from Blackpool beach one on top of the other, the RSPCA would arrest you for animal cruelty and you'd do serious time.

• Every day the rides on the Pleasure Beach result in the production of 33 litres of vomit. That's enough to fill a bath tub! Not that I've checked.

QUICK FACTS Blackpool

Number of Glaswegians in Blackpool right now: 37,000.

Number of stag parties in Blackpool right now: 67,370.

Number of hen parties in Blackpool right now: 67,370.

Number of Northern paternity tests in the next month: 67,370.

Number of visitors wearing polo shirts with 'Bazza' printed on the back: 182.

Number of lightbulbs in the illuminations: at least 138 (I lost count after that).

GLASGOW

HISTORY

The city of Glasgow started life as a tiny religious community founded ages ago by Saint Mungo. That was the same bloke who went on to set up a London-based homeless charity, which tells you a lot about the sort of folk you find in Glasgow. He also appeared in the film *Blazing Saddles* and I think he's also the one with an afro who sang 'In the Summertime', which is weird because Glasgow doesn't really have a summertime, just a slightly less rainy week in June.

Daniel Defoe, writing his apparently famous book *A Tour Through the Whole Island of Great Britain,* visited Glasgow ages ago and had this to say about it:

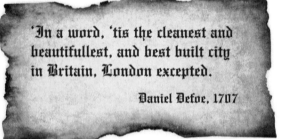

'In a word, 'tis the cleanest and beautifullest, and best built city in Britain, London excepted.

Daniel Defoe, 1707

First of all, that isn't in a word – it's in thirteen words, one of which Daniel's obviously made up. Secondly, the comment doesn't carry that much weight, bearing in mind he seems to like London. And thirdly, what's a baddy from *Spiderman* doing writing travel books? Based on that little sample, he should probably just stick to being the Green Goblin.

Anyway, they may mostly look like Taggart, but the people of Glasgow are a hard-working lot who spent most of the Victorian era building bloody great boats. There's nothing more Northern than building boats, and Glasgow built more than the rest of the country put together, which is going some.

Nowadays, people don't need as many boats so Glaswegians spend their time drinking Tennents, watching football and getting into fights. Football's a bit of a hot potato because everyone – *everyone* – there supports either Rangers or Celtic (depending on whether they like the Pope or not), and matches can sometimes get a bit lively. But visitors looking for a scrap, beware – the Scots regularly throw trees around for fun, they actually *like* drinking whisky, AND often wear skirts in temperatures that would have even a Geordie reaching for a jumper. They're double-hard bastards who would likely give Steven Seagal a run for his money. Or probably just mug him for it.

When not at football matches or fighting (or both), Glaswegians are at home practising the art of becoming a premiership football manager.

ATTRACTIONS

• **GLASGOW NECROPOLIS** This is an enormous and apparently famous graveyard near the city centre which contains loads of fancy tombs for people I've never heard of. More importantly, it's a great place to go for some quiet reflection – and it's about the only place in Glasgow where you won't get into a fight. Though that's not a guarantee, they'll fight anywhere.

• **WELLPARK BREWERY** Founded in 1740, this is something of a Mecca for Glaswegians (well, when one of the two Mecca Bingos in the town centre isn't open anyway) because it's where Tennents is made. Fans of Scotland's number one tipple can often be found gathered outside the brewery shouting 'Ah'm better'n this', pestering passers-by for change and vomiting into the bins. Admittedly, the brewery doesn't look all that nice and it can often get a bit nippy round there, but a couple of cans of Tennents Super will keep Jack Frost at bay.

For maximum efficiency, the Wellpark Brewery backs straight on to the Glasgow Necropolis.

Fun fact: it's actually quite hard to organise a piss-up in this particular brewery because they don't let members of the public in. ≫→

*"Gordon Brown was the one with one eye who was **Prime Minister** after the one with the teeth."*

• **EDINBURGH** Just fifty miles right of Glasgow along the M8 is the beautiful city of Edinburgh. Steeped in history with a picturesque town centre and lots of friendly locals, Edinburgh is everything Glasgow isn't. Except when it's flooded with southern comedians in search of the true rhythm of comedy (people are laughing, job done), or Rangers and Celtic are playing, because then it's awash with Glaswegians.

FAMOUS GLASWEGIANS

• **MARK KNOPFLER** As lead guitarist for Dire Straits, Mark Knopfler has the fastest hands in the world and has insured each finger for £1 billion (excluding thumbs). Mark did the twiddly bits on 'Calling Elvis' and has done more for bandana-wearing than anyone – with the exception, perhaps, of Bruce Springsteen, Keith Richards, Axl Rose, Eminem and pirates.

• **ROBBIE COLTRANE** This world-famous American-be-bop-saxophonist-turned-Scottish-criminal-psychologist has worked with all the greats: Thelonious Monk, Miles Davis, Daniel Radcliffe and James Bond. You don't see him playing the sax very much these days, but *Cracker* was proper good so I don't really mind. They say the camera adds ten pounds in weight and it's only because Robbie's been on TV so much that he looks as big as a house.

• **SIR ALEX FERGUSON** Has had a modicum of sporting success by telling footballers where to stand and which direction to kick the ball in.

• **GORDON BROWN** He was the one with the eye who was Prime Minister after the one with the teeth. May or may not be responsible for bringing the Universe to the brink of financial collapse or pulling the Universe back from the brink of financial collapse or both or neither. Met Barack Obama once and hangs out with J. K. Rowling.

• **GORDON RAMSAY** The other famous Glaswegian Gordon. But the less said about this so-called Northerner, the better – see page 172 for details of his Crimes Against the North.

> *"Glasgow's climate is affectionately known as '**shit**' by the rest of the world."*

LOCAL TRIVIA

• Glasgow is twinned with both Bethlehem and Lahore, which I can only assume is them hedging their bets when it comes to the Almighty.

• Some Glaswegians play a sport called Shinty, which is basically a big scrap with sticks.

• People hailing from Glasgow are affectionately known as 'scum' by the rest of Scotland.

• Glasgow's climate is affectionately known as 'shit' by the rest of the world.

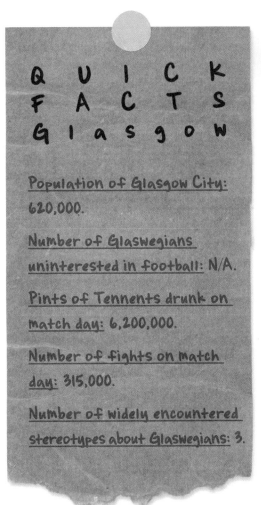

QUICK FACTS Glasgow

Population of Glasgow City: 620,000.

Number of Glaswegians uninterested in football: N/A.

Pints of Tennents drunk on match day: 6,200,000.

Number of fights on match day: 315,000.

Number of widely encountered stereotypes about Glaswegians: 3.

GUIDE TO **WORKING** MEN'S CLUBS

{ Entrance at the rear ☞ }

DRIFFIELD DRINKERS & SMOKING MEN'S CLUB

This charming venue manages to combine small-town charm with a big-city feel. Known for its bold and daring architecture, 'The Driff' is loosely themed around 'brown' and decorated throughout with car-boot sale chic, nicotine-stained Formica and a pre-war beige carpet. A haven of calm in the hustle and bustle of busy Driffield, the club does suffer from a lack of natural light, customers and working toilets. Women are not welcome in the tap room.

Facilities: A door.

Entertainment: Pool table (missing white ball, one cue), bar billiards (no cues), Krypton Factor fruit machine but the coin slot can be a tad unreliable.

Ambience: Underfunded municipal library cum hospital ward.

Likelihood of a fight: 32%.

Interesting fact: The condom-vending machine dispenses ribbed for her pleasure; the fruit machine dispenses tokens for the condom machine (but only if you hit the jackpot).

Biggest acts to date: In 2004, Andy Abraham popped in to try and use the toilets. But they weren't working so he left.

WAKEFIELD DRINKING, SMOKING & FIGHTING MEN'S CLUB

Despite the name, this bijou little club in the Latin quarter of Wakefield plays host to no sport. What's more, since their electricity was cut off in 2007, they can't even show sporting events on the bracket-mounted 20in TV. But the total absence of artificial light, piped music and running water simply add to the charm. The more 'traditional' visitor may be delighted to discover the venue has a 'relaxed' attitude to the country-wide ban on smoking and the proprietor is also jauntily ambivalent towards underage drinkers. Best avoided when a man known as 'The Toothfairy' is drinking there.

Facilities: two bars, a dining room, four stools.

Entertainment: Ella behind the bar, arrows.

Ambience: Simmering tension tinged with despair.

Likelihood of a fight: 0% (rising to 100% if 'The Toothfairy' is in).

Highlight: The car park.

Biggest acts to date: Keith Harris & Cuddles (Keith in 1984, Cuddles in 1985).

PRUDHOE DRINKING & SWEARING MEN'S CLUB

'Not Newcastle', as it's affectionately referred to by Geordies, is often overlooked by visitors to the North-East of England. But Prudhoe's lack of travellers, tourists, backpackers or anyone under the age of seventy simply adds to its appeal for the discerning working-man tourist. Prudhoe Drinking & Swearing Men's Club really is the highlight of this town – there can be few better views of the B6395 than from the club's main bar (although the term 'main bar' is a little misleading, implying some sort of choice). The enchanting decor and intriguing aroma make this venue a real gem.

Facilities: Male 'AND' female toilet.

Entertainment: Chess board (queens missing), fire extinguisher.

Ambience: Youth club without the youth.

Likelihood of a fight: 10%, unless it's 'Fight Night' (day varies).

Last burnt down: 2006 (arson/insurance).

Biggest acts to date: According to a plaque in the bar, Ted Rogers called the Prudhoe Drinking & Swearing Men's Club phone by accident in 1983.

ACCRINGTON NOT CONSERVATIVE MEN'S CLUB

This compact and boutique destination offers a welcome antidote to some of the larger, more impersonal clubs in the area. Constructed entirely from wood in the back garden of club chairman Mr Adrian Scotney, the club exercises a lax approach to the 'members only' rule and has a capacity of eight. Completists may like to know that Accrington Not Conservative Men's Club & Shed (to give it its full name) is completely exempt from the constraints of UK licensing laws (according to Adrian). No swearing, no naked flames, no drinking the paint stripper.

Facilities: Lots of paint, two spades and a lawnmower.

Entertainment: Wind-up radio with a coathanger for an aerial.

Ambience: Pine-fresh.

Likelihood of a fight: 0% (according to Adrian).

Founded: 1286 (according to Adrian).

Biggest acts to date: U2, PopMart Tour '97 (according to Adrian).

HORWICH DRINKING & FIGHTING MEN'S CLUB

This cosmopolitan establishment shares its main entrance with a sexual health centre, making it both easy to find and difficult to enter. However, once past the embarrassed-people-scratching queue, the HDFMC is a haven of calm with low-lighting, minimalist decoration and three for one on all spirits. The bar serves a selection of drinks – none of them labelled or readily recognisable – and the staff have a unique approach to customer service. Tradition is clearly important in the HDFMC and pre-decimal currency is still accepted here.

Facilities: First aid kit, 'Test Your Sex Drive' machine.

Entertainment: Telling everyone about your mate whos's in the clinic next door.

Ambience: Clinical yet dirty.

Likelihood of a fight: 75%, dropping considerably once the STI clinic opens.

Founded: Bring your own mixers.

Biggest acts to date: Steve Brookstein stayed for a few nights earlier this year (in Horwich. Not in the Club. Or the clinic).

81

TOP TRAMPS

FATHER PISSEDMASS

Real name unknown, so the local kids nicknamed him Father Pissedmass, due to his uncanny resemblance to Santa.

HOMETOWN: Bolton	**100/100**
TIPPLE: Any white spirit	**20/100**
SCENT: Pine needles & corpse	**95/100**
CATCHPHRASE: 'Merry f**kin Christmas, yer f**kin b***ard yer!!!'	**100/100**
LOCATION: Bus station	**75/100**
SOB STORY: 'That slag took everything!'	**45/100**
ADI (average daily income): £2.56, handful of mistletoe	**60/100**

JEDWOODS

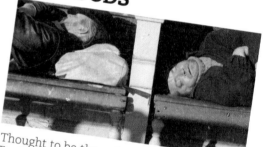

Thought to be the only homeless twins in England. They are called Jedwoods (a witty reference to the *X Factor* failures) because one of them is called Jed and they live in the woods.

HOMETOWN: Saddleworth	**10/100**
TIPPLE: Turps	**100/100**
SCENT: Wet dog	**80/100**
CATCHPHRASE: 'We've got the Z factor'	**75/100**
LOCATION: Various woodlands	**5/100**
SOB STORY: 'Those whores took everything!'	**100/100**
ADI: Nuts and berries	**5/100**

MAD DOUGY

Although he's madder than toast, Mad Dougy is very camera shy.

HOMETOWN: Durham	80/100
TIPPLE: Vinegar (Netto brand)	85/100
SCENT: Urine & biscuits	60/100
CATCHPHRASE: 'Gravy makes me laugh'	90/100
LOCATION: Various hospital outpatients	20/100
SOB STORY: 'That bitch took everything!'	35/100
ADI: 86p, half a packet of Hobnobs	15/100

DENZEL NEEDS-A-WASHINGTON

Denzel can be found roaming the streets of Liverpool, quoting lines from the movie *The Pelican Brief*.

HOMETOWN: Liverpool	75/100
TIPPLE: Rum & medicine	90/100
SCENT: Yeast infection	100/100
CATCHPHRASE: 'I've won an Oscar laaaa'	60/100
LOCATION: Toxteth shopping arcade	80/100
SOB STORY: 'She took everything, she did though, didn't she though!'	10/100
ADI: £5.99, two aspirin and a bag of chips	100/100

PAUL

Paul is one of Top Tramps' youngest entrants. His piss-addled looks belie his twenty-five years. Paul is quite the high-flying yuppie of the homeless world.

HOMETOWN: Skegness	35/100
TIPPLE: Home(less) Brew	75/100
SCENT: Brut & spew	55/100
CATCHPHRASE: 'I tell ya, I'm only 25! Buy, buy, buy, sell!'	20/100
LOCATION: Outside the wine bar of Skegness	40/100
SOB STORY: 'The cow left me, didn't believe I was twenty-five!'	65/100
ADI: £12.50 and a broken Nokia	100/100

TARQUIN

Tarquin is the poorest, most destitute tramp in the whole of the south.

HOMETOWN: Winchester	0/100
TIPPLE: Pimms & lemonade	1/100
SCENT: Mink & Joan Collins	0/100
CATCHPHRASE: 'One is feeling awfully squiffy, what, what!'	0/100
LOCATION: Henley Regatta, Cowes or any royal polo match	0/100
SOB STORY: 'The Duchess took a reasonable proportion of everything I inherited!'	1/100
ADI: £1.2m (interest payments on trust fund)	0/100

STORIES FROM PADDY'S YOUTH... 📖

When I was a lad, growing up was all about adventure. Me and my mates would spend endless summers out and about exploring, making up games, and creating our own fun. These days, though, it's all PlayBox 320 this, and Nintendo MegaWee that; kids don't know what fresh air is. It's not their fault, mind – it's the politicians with all their safe and healthy laws that say you can't do this, shouldn't do that, not allowed to go here, mustn't inject that... It gets on my you-know-whats because playing outside never did me any harm. I've got so many stories from my days as a lad, that's a whole other book (note to publishers: I'm serious), but here are just a few to give you a taste of what it was like growing up in the North in the ~~seventies~~ *eighties*

The day Foggy, Edgey, Lowther and me played hide-and-seek at the dump

We didn't have playgrounds where I grew up. Well, we did have one, but this beardy bloke called Frank the Fiddler always hung around the swings, so we gave that a miss. Any rate, the dump was much more fun. Me and my mates would climb through a hole in the fence and play ninjas with sharp stuff we found from the scrap metal pile until the sun went down. Or until the bloke who drove the hydraulic car-crusher chased us away, whichever came first. Anyway, this one time, we were rooting about in the household appliance hopper when Foggy suggested a game of hide-and-seek. It wasn't until later we realised it was because Foggy had found an excellent hiding place. Much later. He was a big lad so it was a wonder he fitted inside that fridge – and even more of a wonder he'd managed to close the door. Anyway, he was quite a lot smaller when the police forensic team eventually found him nine days later. On the plus side though, he thrashed us at the game and still holds the 'Bolton Hide 'n' Seek' championship medal.

The day Edgey, Lowther, Iqbal and me found the secret mine

Edgey's big brother always claimed he'd discovered a disused mine full of jazz mags somewhere out in the countryside. These days, those sort of unsafe structures are easy to spot because they're surrounded by barbed-wire fences and yellow danger signs, but back then there was none of that – you just had to go looking. One day we all decided to go off in search of the mythical porn mine so we packed a pork pie, a can of Shandy Bass and a Curly Wurly and set off on our epic adventure. Two hours later, Iqbal was busy spewing up after finding out that the pork pies were in fact not Halal. We decided to abort mission and head home for our tea when Iqbal disappeared from view. The lucky bugger's spew had only dissolved a makeshift lid which had been covering the entrance to the porno mine shaft! It took mountain rescue a couple of hours to locate Iqbal, by which time he'd passed out after choking on his own vomit. At the time Lowther, Edgey and myself were more upset to learn they hadn't found ANY porn down there. Edgey's brother eventually admitted he'd made that bit up.

The day Edgey, Lowther and me played Danger Frisbee

Frisbee was for girls and blokes who wet themselves in assembly. Danger Frisbee, on the other hand – that was for men. Admittedly, it was me who invented the rules of Danger Frisbee and we only played it once, but it was a proper sport. The idea was to take turns lobbing a frisbee as hard as possible into the overhead power lines that ran behind Texas Homecare. Whoever wedged it in the pylons first, got to send the other one up to get the frisbee down. Long story short, my wicked kung-fu throws meant Edgey and Lowther ended up climbing the pylon. That day, I learned a lot about electricity, and my mates learned a lot about electrical burns and Danger Frisbee.

After that summer, no one seemed to want to sit next to me at school, but I think that was because I was so good-looking. My striking good looks can be intimidating. Still, happy days...

NORTHERN
GUIDE
TO FILM

Dave The Oracle once told me that going to the pictures will become a thing of the past when every home up here in the North has a telly in it. Well, I can't see that happening! A telly in every home? Get your head out of the clouds, son, we can't all be Richard Branson.

So until the impossible happens, us Northerners will keep on going to the cinema. Oh yes, there's nothing we enjoy more than spending a week's wages on a hot dog and having teenagers flick Maltesers at us from the row behind while trying to watch a movie.

To celebrate this fact, I went down to the Odeon in Bolton to check out some of the very latest releases. As I'm friendly with the owner, Terry, he's let me in after hours to have a sneaky advanced look at some of the very latest releases. So here is my inside scoop on the hot new films that are premiering in the North very soon.

UNDER SIEGE

*Starring Steven Seagal
and Erika Eleniak*

I've always thought that my ultimate film would star Steven Seagal, contain amazing fights and a tiny bit of breast exposure from a *Baywatch* lass. But this film goes one better than I could've imagined in my wildest dreams – it's got a giant cake in it too! And I love cake just as much as I love breasts, fights and Sir Steven.

Not only is the plot of *Under Siege* incredible, it also contains an ingenious twist – a twist you will never see coming in a million years. Some mercenaries storm an American battleship and take all the naval officers hostage. BUT! They didn't bank on the fact that, and here comes the twist, the ship's cook (Steven Seagal) is a former Navy Seal. Honestly, you couldn't make this stuff up. But they have – somehow. The cook! That's the last thing the mercenaries would expect.

Under Siege will be the movie that catapults Seagal on to a whole new level. Mark my words, once the public see this film, Seagal will become so huge he'll be able to leave action movies and have a career in politics. I could easily see him as governor of California in the next decade. I'd love to see a sequel to *Under Siege*, maybe set on some form of transport other than a boat. Just imagine.

FIGHT FACTOR: **10/10**

SEAGAL FACTOR: **10/10**

TITILLATION FACTOR: **7/10**
(topless cake surprise, some French kissing)

OVERALL: **10/10**

INDECENT PROPOSAL

Starring Robert Redford, Woody Harrelson and Demi Moore

If you like fights and Steven Seagal, you're in for a disappointment here. All that happens in this film is Robert Redford pays Woody Harrelson a million dollars to sleep with his missus. Obviously to make the film last a bit longer, there's a lot of um-ing and ah-ing that also goes on but, to be honest, I don't know why they all spend so much time navel-gazing. It's not a difficult decision really – a million dollars for sleeping with Robert Redford? For that kind of money, I'll bloody do it.

This film could really have done with some kind of twist. Something like: just as Robert Redford and Demi Moore are about to do the deed, a bellboy bursts into the hotel room and turns out to be an ex-Navy Seal and he defeats Redford in a knife fight and he saves Demi Moore. Because the last person you'd expect is the bellboy, isn't it?

In real life, Demi Moore is married to Bruce Willis and in this film she gets busy with Robert Redford. So one thing's for sure – she's only got an eye for the older man. So no danger of her getting herself a toy boy.

FIGHT FACTOR: **0/10**

SEAGAL FACTOR: **0/10**

TITILLATION FACTOR: **2/10**
(bra strap removal, bit of fully clothed thrusting)

OVERALL: **2/10**

WATERWORLD

....

Starring Kevin Costner

Kevin Costner can do no wrong! And the cinema-going public are going to lap this one up. I can see *Waterworld* turning into a movie franchise bigger than *Star Wars* – there are going to be sequels upon sequels of this amazing movie!

OK, so it would have been nice to see a role for a true action star (e.g. Steven Seagal) in there somewhere plus a bit more knife/corkscrew fighting. However, the lack of this is more than made up for with some beltin' jet-ski stunts.

The only problem I have with this movie is the implausible plot. Do they expect us to believe that one day it will be possible for the ice caps to melt and then the sea levels to rise? What a lot of bollocks! This is the talk of scaremongering hedge-witches. And what's more, my pals all agreed with me as we discussed the film over a few beers sat round some burning tyres to keep us warm.

FIGHT FACTOR: **0/10**

JET-SKI FACTOR: **10/10**

SEAGAL FACTOR: **0/10**

TITILLATION FACTOR: **4/10**
(post-apocalyptic bikinis)

OVERALL: **8/10**

FREE FIVER

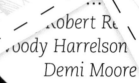

... ...obert Re...
...oody Harrelson...
Demi Moore

...ghts and Steven Seagal, you're in for a disappointment ... that happens in this film is Robert Redford pays Woody ...relson a million dollars to sleep with his missus. Obviously to make the film last a bit longer, there's a lot of um-ing and ah-ing that also goes on but, to be honest, I don't know why they all spend so much time navel-gazing. It's not a difficult decision really – a million dollars for sleeping with Robert Redford? For that kind of money, I'll bloody do it.

This film could really have done with some kind ... Something like: just as Robert Redford and De... about to do the deed, a bellboy bursts into th... turns out to be an ex-Navy Seal and he ... ...ife fight and he saves Demi Moore ... you'd ...

.../10

Life's not been unkind to me over the last few years so I thought I'd take this opportunity to spread the wealth. In EVERY copy of this book is a FREE five pound note! All you need to do is cut out the fiver above – assuming one of those cheeky scamps at our Liverpool printing press hasn't got there before you! Just kidding.

No, seriously – they're good lads. They wouldn't do a thing like that, honest as the day is long. Now take your fiver and buy yourself something nice.

NORTHERN·HEADLINES

Northern local journalism is second to none. Admittedly, I've never read local papers from anywhere else, but I'm pretty sure that the regional press here is better than anywhere else in the world. It's that combination of brilliant writing and a clear big-picture perspective on what really matters. So, as a tribute to local Northern papers, here's my pick of the front pages from some of the most important dates in history.

· PRINCESS DIANA ·

PRESTON ECHO – August 31st 1997

PRINCESS DEAD
Preston's 'Dog of the Year' Killed
By Ian Pegram

The whole of Preston was in mourning today when it was announced that four-times winner of 'Preston's Dog of the Year' has died. Golden retriever Princess caught the imagination of the Lancashire public with her warm personality and beauty, which helped to win her the first of those four titles back in 1993.

CAR ACCIDENT

Princess's untimely death was the result of a terrible car accident which occurred at the climax of a high-speed chase; Princess had been chasing cars all afternoon. She was rushed to a nearby veterinarian's, but they pronounced her dead on arrival and then charged her owners £450 for the privilege.

INQUEST

An inquest into the circumstances surrounding Princess's death has been launched which aims to get to the bottom of rumours about the killer car's French driver, who some believe was over the drink drive limit.

ELTON JOHN TRIBUTE

Princess's owner Mrs Linda Harrison has already penned a tribute song to her beloved dog, based on an Elton John song. The song will be released to raise money for dogs with addictions to vehicular pursuit (car chasing) and is entitled 'Don't Go Breaking My Legs (With Your Car)'.

ROYAL CAR PRANG

A member of the royal family got themselves into a spot of bother today in Paris. For full story, turn to *page 52*.

BURY EVENING NEWS
September 11th 2001

THE DARKEST DAY

Bury FC suffer sixth successive defeat - *By Pete Rudden*

September the 11th, 2001, will be seared into the collective consciousness as one of the most catastrophic days in history after Bury FC slumped to yet another defeat in League One. This is now officially one of the worst starts to a season Bury have ever had.

NEW YORK INCIDENT

A couple of office blocks got into a spot of bother in New York today. For full story, turn to *page 37.*

UTTER CARNAGE

It was utter carnage as The Shakers lost 1–0 to Wrexham. Hopes of Bury breaking a five-match losing streak crumbled to the ground in tiny pieces, leaving bystanders open-mouthed in shock.

SURPRISE ATTACK

The goal itself came from a surprise attack resulting in Lee Trundle scoring the only goal of the match – and in doing so, immediately becoming public enemy number one. His 84th-minute winner broke the hearts of the travelling Bury fans.

COUNTLESS INJURIES

To add insult to injury, several Bury players picked up knocks which may rule them out of next Saturday's game. Most notably, Bury defender Matt Barrass picked up a potentially serious knee problem and was stretchered off part way through the match.

TRIBUTES PAID

In the aftermath of the disaster, Bury boss Andy Preece offered some words of consolation: 'The lads gave it everything and I'm sure things will turn if we keep playing like that.'

Disaster Strikes New York
New York Carpet Emporium goes up in flames

By **Dougy Watchman**

Today is a very dark day for Billy Rugs, owner of New York Carpet Emporium. The business he built up from scratch, along with its sister company, Wall to Wall Street Laminates, today went up in flames.

VISCOSE THE LOT

Firefighters are still investigating what actually caused the blaze. Some experts are claiming that it was an accident waiting to happen. Jack Redmond from the institute of man-made fibres said: 'To keep a roll of polypropylene and acrylic shag so close to a radiator was asking for trouble. All this, along with a viscose-based stair carpet and a no smoking ban in the shop being lifted, was always going to end in tears, along with chemical burns.'

BIG APPLE WILL NEVER BE THE SAME

New York carpets will also be sorely missed by all the OAPs in the area. Tuesdays were mad busy after Billy introduced the Big Apple coffee mornings for the elderly and infirm. Edna Butler, 86, loved her Tuesdays in New York. 'Mr Rugs made sure that me and the other girls were well looked after. He used to make us all a nice cup of coffee and even helped out by taking all our pension books off us for safe keeping, to pay for the carpets he'd sold to us.'

FRAUD

Billy Rugs isn't a stranger to drama as he was acquitted for fraud and illegal money lending in June of last year. Mr Rugs was delighted to have his name cleared and even offered to have the courtroom fitted out with a 60 x 80 wool mix, all this along with 25% off friends and family rate.

A RIGHT KICK IN THE BOLLOCKS

Mr Rugs spoke briefly to one of our reporters. 'Excuse the pun, but the rug has well and truly been pulled from under my feet. This is a right kick in the bollocks, especially as the coffee mornings had just got going. It's a shame that all those old ladies pension books, along with any incriminating receipts, have all gone up in smoke.'

Irony As New York Actually Does Go Up In Flames!

(New York night club Leeds also on fire) Full story page 8.

**SUNDERLAND CHRONICLE –
July 20th 1969**

ONE GIANT LEAP

SUNDERLAND MAN JUMPS OVER TWO VANS

By Stuart Bootland

Everyone in Sunderland will remember exactly where they were when they saw stunt motorcyclist Eddie Armstrong jump over two vans: on Fawcett Street. Because that's where the feat took place.

HISTORICAL LANDING

Eddie launched himself from a home-made ten-foot-high ramp and, upon landing, became the first man ever to have jumped over two vans on a motorcycle within Sunderland's town limits (the feat has been achieved in nearby Washington, but never in Sunderland).

'ONE SMALL STEP'

Eddie was understandably extremely proud of his achievement. He commented, 'This ain't like taking one small step, man, this is like taking one fooking massive gigantic leap over a couple of vans on a motorbike, man, pet.'

TOWN BROUGHT TO STANDSTILL

The whole of Sunderland came to a standstill during Eddie's incredible achievement – due to people wanting to watch his historic stunt, but mainly due to the fact Fawcett Street had to be closed while he performed his daring act. Eddie is already looking ahead to his next stunt: 'I'm gonna go one better and jump two vans and a moped, pet.'

AMERICAN NERDS IN SPACE

American science geeks put a flag in a bit of gigantic space rock today. For full story, turn to *page 46*.

SOUTHERNERS – HOW TO SPOT
A NORTHERNER

The North of England is a rich tapestry lovingly spread over an ever-changing landscape and woven from the many and varied fibres of different communities, cultures, traditions, and other words like that. Of course the south is pretty much one big city in which people eat raw fish, pay for things in microchips, and wouldn't pour a latte on you if you were on fire.

On some sad occasions a Northerner may accidentally stray into this strange and unwelcoming land. So to any southerners who have stopped eating hummus for long enough to read this page, here are my top ten, foolproof (and they have to be for you lot) telltale signs that you've got a Northerner in your midst:

How-do

1 If someone approaches you in the street, offers a friendly 'How-do!', 'Hey-up!', 'Alreet!' or simply 'Hello', then enquires after the time, they are not about to nick your wallet. They're a Northerner. Don't get your butler to report, sue or shoot them. Just tell them the time, comment on the weather, and be on your merry way.

2 When in a wine lodge, a swanky club, a hotel bar or the one remaining pub in the south, should you overhear a confused gentleman inquiring of the barman 'How much? Let me get this straight – that's for ONE pint?', my friend, you have a Northerner. I've seen houses up here cheaper than your pints.

3 Should you be out for a business-dinner or power-lunch – or whatever you call it – with a colleague and they show little interest in the snail soup, sea urchin vapour or goat's cheese tart flavoured chicken's tongue and instead just wants a pie – a meat pie with pastry and meat inside – then they're a Northerner. Meat pies should never, ever be off the menu. Except perhaps after a funeral. Actually, scratch that. A good pie makes for a good wake.

4 A young man who tries to steal your wallet with an expressionless look on his face is a common thief. A young man who refers to you as 'our kid', flashes a cheeky grin, and then tries to steal your wallet is a Northerner. As well as being a thief.

5 If someone refers to Leicester, Birmingham or Chesterfield as 'down south' don't be alarmed – it's just a Northerner. If someone refers to Carlisle, Edinburgh or Inverness as 'down south', that is cause for alarm – it's a Scot.

6 A fight is a perfectly acceptable and civil way to settle disputes and assert authority in the North. If this option is presented to you down south, just look upon it as bonding with a Northerner.

GROSSBRITANNIEN

7 In 'winter', when you southerners like to wear 'coats' and 'gloves' to stop the 'sleet' and 'snow' from causing 'frostbite', don't be alarmed to see a fella in a T-shirt, smart slacks and slip-ons; he's a Northerner. Instead of pointing and staring, do him a favour and buy him a Calippo – he's probably burning up.

8 Someone who (quite rightly) thinks that dinner is at midday, supper is in the evening, tea is at teatime, and none of them consist of two parsnip crisps and a soya milk chai tea, is a Northerner.

9 If someone's toasting their newborn baby with a pint of bitter and some mates, that could be a southern father. If someone's toasting their newborn baby with a pint of bitter and some mates *whilst the baby's being born* – that's a Northern father. Or a Northern surgeon.

10 Sport is a useful topic for identifying Northerners: fans of cricket, tennis, golf, badminton, hockey, croquet, squash, table tennis, polo, swimming, softball, fives, archery, whiff-whaff, fencing, rowing, cycling, judo, sailing, basketball, bridge or Manchester United are not Northerners. Everyone else is.

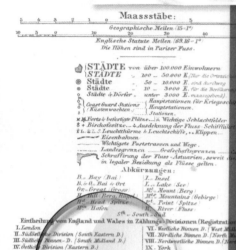

As I think I've made pretty clear by now, the North of England is much better than the south. Thankfully, most southerners haven't realised that yet or they'd all be traipsing up here and taking our jobs and our whippets.

But you do sometimes get the odd plucky southerner testing his mettle and heading North of the border – normally either for a bet or because they've gone the wrong way on the M1.

So if you spot someone acting strangely in Stockport, weirdly in Wakefield, or like a loony in Lidl, don't call the funny farm and get them strapped to a gurney for the rest of their natural life. Check them against my ten telltale signs of a southerner and see if they are, in fact, from down there. If they are, then you can call the funny farm and get them strapped to a gurney for the rest of their natural life. (Trust me – it's more humane than sending them back to Notting Hill.) OK, here goes:

1 Those people you find lying down outside an estate agents' aren't tramps, they're southerners. If you're really lucky, you might catch the moment when one of them takes a glance at the property prices in the North and collapses in shock; it all happens in seconds. Thankfully, there are specially trained clean-up teams who go around every Northern town nightly to collect them all up and post them back to their reassuringly over-priced London flats.

2 The only thing that should go into a pint of beer is more beer (and occasionally a finger when carrying). Nothing good will ever come of adding lemonade, lime cordial or ice cubes, and only a southerner would suggest such a thing.

3 If you're out on the town of an evening sometime in the middle of second-summer (November to March) and you spot a man or woman with way too many clothes on wandering about the club asking for something called 'the cloakroom', they're southern. According to Dave The Oracle, in and around London the 'cloakroom' is a tiny, one-room club built inside another club. Apparently it costs £2 to get in, but what goes on in there is anyone's business – every time Dave tried to get close, the queue was so long he just gave up and went back to the main club bar. (Note: If the person asking for the 'cloakroom' has an American accent then they're probably an American, and are in fact asking for the lav. Don't confuse the two.)

4 Should you overhear anyone use the words 'vegan option', 'wheat-free', 'organic', 'lactose-intolerant', 'carbohydrate', 'nut allergy', 'protein', 'soya', 'omega oils', 'vitamin', 'vegetable' or 'cutlery' in the Chippy, the curry house – or in fact anywhere – then they're definitely southern. Not even they know what all those things mean. 'Ooo! I can't have milk – it doesn't agree with me!' Shut up and eat your Choco Rocks!

5 Flat caps, overalls and hobnail boots are worn by Northerners; novelty cufflinks, moleskin shoulder-bags and diamond-weave golfing thin-knits are not. Not even at fancy-dress parties.

6 Anyone with intimate knowledge of (and a keen interest in discussing) the M2, the M3, the M4, the M5, the M11, the M20, the M23, the M25, the M26, the M27, the M32, the M40, the M50, the M271 or the M275 is a southerner. Anyone with intimate knowledge of (and a keen interest in discussing) an M16 or an M60 is probably a gun-smuggler or a terrorist. Both sorts of people are best avoided.

7 When greeting someone, if they call you 'old bean', 'Northern oik' or 'butler', then that's a southerner. If they also add in a few racist remarks about piccaninnies or say something offensive about Scousers, then that's Boris Johnson. He's what I call a 'double southerner'.

8 A person pointing along any street in any Northern town and asking 'Is this where Coronation Street is filmed?' is a southerner. Coronation Street is of course filmed on a very detailed and realistic-looking set built inside Granada Studios. All Northerners know that... except for the people who live there (or, as we know them, 'the cast') – they think it's 100% real.

9 Anyone expecting any more than three types of drink (tea, coffee, pop) to be on offer anywhere is definitely a southerner.

10 Sport is a useful topic for identifying southerners: fans of Bolton Wanderers, Burnley FC and Manchester City are clearly Northern; fans of rugby, cricket, tennis, golf, badminton, hockey, croquet, squash, polo, swimming, softball, fives, archery, whiff-whaff, fencing, rowing, cycling, sailing, basketball, bridge or Manchester United are not.

Southern PIONEERS

Now I may have had a bit of fun with our southern cousins so far, but obviously those were just harmless jokes. Humour aside, it's time to get serious. So I have devoted some pages to celebrating the true pioneers from the south. These are the southerners who are bravely stepping out into uncharted territory to push back the boundaries within their specialised fields, so that we as a society can move forward. Here are the southern pioneers we must learn from if the North is ever to progress.

BOBBY DAVRO
COMEDIAN

Now here is a man on the cutting edge of comedy. Heavily influenced by American comics like Lenny Bruce and Richard Prior, Bobby worked his way up through the alternative comedy scene, always flaunting controversy with his risqué take-offs of underground icons of the time such as Sooty and Frank Spencer. His routines were well ahead of their time. Up until Davro, people had only been doing recognisable impressions of celebrities, but Bobby changed all that. He realised that the audience didn't necessarily want accuracy – they wanted 'vaguely recognisable' impressions. He was doing this over twenty years before Dead Ringers used the same idea. A bona fide genius.

ERIC RICKSWORTH
INVENTOR

This name may not mean a lot to you, but this man was the greatest inventor of our time. That's right. Ricksworth was the creator of Babestation, Babestation 2 and Get Lucky TV. I remember the first day Babestation started. Everyone in my footy team rushed into their homes and tuned in. We had street parties. It was a good time. Of course the first broadcaster on the channel was old Dani O'Neal, and who could imagine TV without her now? She really is the Richard Whiteley of Babestation. Much like the reaction to Channel 4's launch, people unfairly called the channel 'smutty'. Luckily, four years on and, with the introduction of Lolly Badcock and Angel Long, the channel is now seen as a much more classy station.

DAVID ICKE
BIOLOGICAL THEORIST

Controversial scientist David Icke is renowned in the south for his breakthrough biological thinking. For years the Pope and Cliff Richard have been trying to sell us some mumbo-jumbo story about a magic man who could walk on water and cure leopards. Well, I've got news for you – it's all a bunch of nonsense. This is the 21st century (hang on there a minute... yep, just checked my sundial, it is the 21st century), and thanks to Mr Icke, we now realise that the world is run by shape-shifting reptilians hell-bent on

microchipping everyone so they can obtain world domination. And that's not me talking – that's science! If you don't believe me, then there's a lot of research to back this up – such as *Tales from the Time Loop* (by David Icke), *Children of the Matrix* (by David Icke) and *Robots Rebellion* (by David Icke). And I know what you're thinking: 'They're all written by David Icke. He could be talking bollocks!' But I ask you this, why would he be talking bollocks when he's the son of God?

SIR DEAN GAFFNEY

ACTOR

Dean is one of the most revered actors of the twentieth century. He grew up learning from his contemporaries – Dame Judi Dench, Sir Ian McKellen and Wellard. Like all the greats, he began his career treading the boards of *The Bill*, where he played that classic character 'Paul Moose', a guy who nicks a thing and gets in trouble for it with the police or something. Unforgettable. He then moved on to work the counter-culture drama *EastEnders*, which received high critical praise from the acting cognoscenti. All of this prepared him for the greatest, and most memorable, role of his life as the character 'Dean Gaffney' in the devised improvisational piece: *I'm A Celebrity... Get Me Out Of Here*. Do try and catch Gaffney at the Old Vic where he is currently performing *Waiting for Godot* with Sir Ian McKellen.

TOPLOADER

BAND

OK, so not all southerners could get to grips with Toploader's challenging musical style when they first came on to the music scene, but over time it has become clear what an incredible and pioneering influence they have had on music. Band members Joseph 'Joey' Washbourn, Dan 'The Man' Hipgrave, Julian Deane (aka Posh-Loader), Rob 'Robson' Green and Matt 'The Bassist' Knight could teach our Northern bands a thing or two about cutting edge music in the 2000s. Back in 1998, Sony records signed the team for a six-album deal – and from that moment on rock music would never be the same again. In a recent poll their renaissance opus 'Achilles Heel' was voted the best song of all time*. The band have been in the studio for the last ten years working on their next album. And as it's taking so long, I'm definite it's going to be an absolute gem. But if you can't wait, then do look out this summer for Ben Elton's new musical *Dancing in the Moonlight* which will include all their greatest hit.

*Results compiled by the Toploader fan club

ALAN SUGAR
BUSINESSMAN

Alan Sugar runs the biggest technology company in the world and he's also the richest man in the universe. His computers are second to none, but in the early eighties he had a lot of competition from another technology giant, Sir Clive Sinclair. Of course we all remember those classic ads: 'Hello. I'm a Sinclair ZX81!', 'And I'm a Amstrad CPC464!' Luckily for Sugar, the Amstrad became the computer of choice and is still used in all major businesses (or at least in every company I've ever worked in). His best move was when the company shocked the world with their revolutionary new phone – the ePhone. It could do all sorts: send email, receive email, make phone calls, receive phone calls... and so much more. Probably. One day I hope that a Northerner will invent something as revolutionary and era-defining as Mr Sugar's ePhone.

C&A
FASHION DESIGNER

Clemens and August Brenninkmeijer are the finest clothing designers on the planet. They design clothes in a whole host of different mediums (ties, slippers, rucksacks... the list is endless). The shop became so exclusive that in the year 2000 they shut all their shops. Now THAT is high class! I have to admit that I'm wearing a C&A outfit now. And yes, it was expensive – £18 for a pair of jeans! But you can't put a price on style. Of course these days you can't buy C&A for love nor money. I assume you'd have to go to Sotheby's to get yourself any of their fine products these days. And I know what you're thinking – you're thinking 'Brenninkmeijer' doesn't sound like a typical southern English name. You're right. I think he's Welsh.

How To Cook Things

With Paddy McGuinness...

The UK is known internationally for its cuisine. From Indian to the good old Chinese takeaway, British food is eaten all around the world. So I thought I'd compile a list of recipes for some of the UK's most exciting and exotic dishes.

As part of my research I've been taking notes from the best regional TV chefs so I can compare and contrast recipes from top Northern cooks, like the Hairy Bikers, with dishes by the traditional southern chefs, like Heston Blumenthal. For those who aren't in the know, Heston's restaurant is very popular with people in the South because they have more money than taste buds.

 The Classic Southern Roast – Northern Style

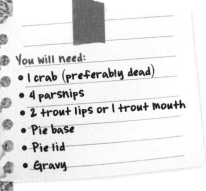

You will need:
- 1 crab (preferably dead)
- 4 parsnips
- 2 trout lips or 1 trout mouth
- Pie base
- Pie lid
- Gravy

1. Take the crab and try and find where the meat is. I couldn't find any, so I dyed some chicken pink instead.

2. Put that in the colander for now (we might need the pan later).

3. Add the parsnips and then take out the parsnips 'cos Heston says you only need the fumes from the parsnip. Then add your trout lips. ≫→

4. I know what you're thinking! Up till now it's just been a direct lift of one of Heston's recipes. But now it's time to put a Paddy twist on it. Listen up Blumenthal, this is how to make your food palatable: pour everything from the colander into your pre-bought pie base. Here's the really important bit: put the pre-bought lid on the pie. It is absolutely key that you do that. Shove the pie in the oven at gas mark "full" – and cook until golden.

5. Meanwhile, microwave the gravy.

6. Then serve with a pint and crisps.

7. Also do make sure that you leave enough space on the plate to remove all of the contents of the pie cos it tastes like overpriced shite.

8. And foursprung dirk technics! There you have it – a perfect south/north fusion Sunday roast.

 ### Chicken Tikka Masala – Northern Style

This dish originates from a place that still practises ancient traditions, a place that's seen epic battles, a place that's home to a whole wealth of dialects. That's right: Birmingham. And the elders of this community have passed the recipe down from generation to generation. That's two generations. They say you can't improve on perfection... but I'm going to try.

You will need:
• 1 microwaveable Chicken Tikka Masala ready meal
• Pie base
• Pie lid
• Gravy

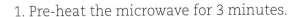

1. Pre-heat the microwave for 3 minutes.

2. Pierce the film on the Chicken Tikka Masala ready meal.

3. Put the plastic tray into the oven and set it for 2 minutes.

Don't put the fork in the microwave. If you do leave it in, remember this next bit: don't film the sparking cutlery with your mobile phone and put it on YouTube. It may look pretty, but trust me – your insurance company will use the video as evidence to decline your claim for a new microwave.

4. Leave it for a minute to cool. Then stir with whatever is close to hand (I used a dog chew). Then put it back in the microwave for another 2 minutes. Try to remember not to leave the dog chew in as this can cause the meal to taste all pig's eary.

5. Now it's time to gild the lily. Take the Chicken Tikka Masala and pour it into the pie base. Place the pie lid firmly on top and put it in the oven. Leave until Corrie's finished.

6. Finally, remove the pie from the oven, add the gravy and serve with Vimto and crisps.

And there you have it! Chicken Tikka Masala à la McGuinness. Note: some pie companies already sell this ready-made but it was my idea I tell ya... miiiiine!!!!

Serving suggestion: serve hot or cold and why not substitute your Vimto with Tizer?

So food fans, there you go! Nigella eat your heart out. And when you do it, don't forget to cover it in pastry and pour over some gravy.

BOLTON HERITAGE

PADDY'S
BLUE PLAQUE
TOUR OF BOLTON

THE STREETS, SCHOOLS AND HOUSES OF THE COMEDIAN & WRITER

If you're casually reading this page while flicking through a dog-eared copy in a charity shop, then stop browsing and go and cough up the fifty pence they're asking for it, you cheapskate. If, however, you've paid good money for this, then here's a little reward in the form of a fact about me: I was born in Bolton.

Bolton is a beautiful town, full to the brim with amazing sights and interesting smells, not to mention fascinating folk both past and present (see 'Dave The Oracle'). Often lumped together with its poorer cousin and satellite village – Manchester – Bolton is very much a destination in its own right and in 2002 was even designated 'Best Place In The World' (by me). Granted, I'd been drinking all day – but what a day it was. So, now you're here, I want to take you on a whistle-stop tour around just a few of the sites of historical and cultural interest that this magnificent medium-sized town has to offer.

NUMBER 26
Auburn Street

This is where I was born and spent those all-important formative years growing up. I can vividly remember the day we moved out – I was thirty-two. The place has clearly had a bit of work done on it since then, although I can't say I'm a fan of this new flash, modern look. You can't see the blue plaque in this photo – mainly because there isn't one. But I'm sure they'll get around to putting it up.

QUEENS PARK
PIE CRUST

This brings back memories! I ended up here after my sixteenth birthday 'party' (which was actually just me, Stotty and Bully drinking cider in the bus station). It was dark, it was windy, I was half-cut and someone had left a life-ring propped up against the wall – all of which tricked my senses into believing I was on the bow of a cross-Channel ferry. All night I was there, clinging on to the 'railing' (wall) for dear life, rocking with the 'waves' (drunkenness), vomiting over the side due to seasickness (again, drunkenness) and occasionally being drenched by 'sea spray' (what that actually was, I'll never know). Over the years the graffiti has come and gone but the old favourites remain. Who needs a blue plaque when you've got 'I **** U' scrawled in red marker pen?

RADCLIFFE ROAD

It's a bit out of town, but everyone in Bolton knows this spot. A true son of Bolton spent many a happy hour here and it's a must-see for anyone with an interest in local history. Because right here, under that blue plaque,

was where I got tops and fingers with Claire Dodson from the year above. Like the fella that used to live in this house, Claire Dodson well and truly demolished my unstable erection.

BOLTON SCHOOL

It's a posh-looking place, but who do you think went here then? Eh? Good-looking bloke – bit of a jack-the-lad, one wonky ear but a hit with the ladies... Yup, you guessed it – Nobel-prize-winning chemist Harry Kroto, world famous for his work on the C60 molecule known as buckminsterfullerene. Well, him and Ralf Little. Maybe those two could share a blue plaque.

HIGH SOCIETY NIGHTCLUB

This is where, after a night on the pop back in '88, Darren Mays got into a fight with Bolton's most famous tramp, Father Pissedmass. Granted, if you don't know Darren Mays then it won't mean much, but trust me – it was worth gathering everyone together and practising that chant. Anyway, Darren went down in the fourth (minute) and Father P. took Dazza's coat, £3.80 in change and one of his shoes as winnings. It was a happier, more innocent time back then; you could happily gamble on tramp fights without the bloody PC brigade getting on your case and accusing you of being inhumane.

NORTHERN
ROYALTY

While Northerners are legally ruled by the British Royal
Family, we also have our own Northern Royal Family. Unlike
Queen Lizzy and her brood, our Royal Family isn't decided
by being born into it. No, a position in our Royal Family is
earned for services to the North. You don't get anything for
nepotism in these parts. It's not a bloody boarding school up
here, you know.

KING SEAN
For the successful worldwide
export of Northern grit

QUEEN LILY
For embodying Northern
femininity

(Sung at 11.15 p.m. every Friday and Saturday in all Northern settlements)

PRINCE NOEL
For composing the Northern National Anthem, 'Wonderwall'

PRINCESS KERRY
For services to frozen food and doner kebabs

PRINCE ANT 'N' DEC
For providing role models to the under-heighted

PRINCESS SUSAN
For achieving what was previously thought to be impossible

(i.e. having a nice-ish singing voice while not looking like a dolly bird)

DUKE PAUL OF LIVERPOOL
For popularising the 'double thumbs-up' gesture

DUCHESS CILLA OF LIVERPOOL
For services to British mating and toothpaste

(i.e. not making a sequel to Spice World)

BARON CHUBBY OF NORTH YORKSHIRE
For lifelong support of the flying helmet and goggles industry and the current British record holder for saying the word 'Piss Flaps' in an hour

BARONESS MEL OF LEEDS
For empowering Northern lasses and for services to British film

DUKE DUKE OF LANCASTER
For reviving the phrase 'bobby dazzler'

(still married to that Madeley fella)

DUCHESS JUDY OF MANCHESTER
For having the patience of a saint

COUNT GAZZA OF NEWCASTLE
For... for... well, for everything he's ever done basically

COUNTESS CHERYL OF NEWCASTLE
For sticking out a few years with Ashley Cole

(would have made Princess but she married that twat Ashley Cole)

DAME JUDI OF YORK
For bossing around that soft southern nancy, James Bond

SIR DANIEL OF CHESHIRE
Despite acting like a soft southern secret agent, for being harder than his even softer Bond predecessor

Cheat's Guide to a...
SOUTHERN PUB QUIZ

Everyone loves a good pub quiz – it's a great way to support your local, make friends, show off how much you know about football, get into a fight with the friends over how much you know about football, and then lose friends again.

But beware of pub quizzes down south. According to Dave The Oracle, they're a little bit different down there – for a start, 'sport' apparently constitutes just one round. And pop culture is laughed at. Laughed at! What else is there? I haven't got a clue, but I know a man who has...

Like a sort of Northern James Bond, Dave The Oracle has secretly infiltrated poncey wine bars all over the south of England and braved this mysterious southern pub quiz so that you don't have to.

What's more, just in case you should find yourself stranded down there with a pint in your hand, an answer sheet on your lap, a quil in the other hand and a sort of empty feeling in your head, Dave The Oracle has prepared the following cheat sheet. If you're going anywhere near the border, take my advice and keep it with you at all times because it'll stop you looking like a divvy when the scores are read out at the end of the quiz.

Geography

A 'geography' round is all to do with countries – but, weirdly, not which ones footballers play for or where that fella Bass Hunter off Celeb BB comes from. Here are the facts you'll need to know:

- There are no countries in the world that start with the letter B.

- Before the Romans discovered Great Britain, it was known simply as 'Not Bad Britain'.

- Coventry is the only town in the UK whose name is the same backwards.

- Rushup Edge in the Peak District is the smallest mountain in the world.

- Brazil in South America took its name from the 1985 Terry Gilliam film *Brazil*; before then it was called 'Brazil' after the Brazil nut.

History

A 'history' round, sadly, does not mean naming every number one from the last five years. But swot up on the following and you can't go wrong:

- The great fire of London was started by a faulty trouser-press in Saville Row.

- The Romans had two stomachs and lived off grass like cows (although they produced no milk).

- Contrary to popular belief, dinosaurs did not speak Latin.

- The year 1066 is famous because it didn't contain an August.

- The Chinese invented tea, but it was the Japanese who invented water.

TV

Again, disappointingly, a TV round will make only scant reference to *Match of the Day* or *Total Wipeout*. So try to memorise these little nuggets:

- Television was invented in 1925 by a Scotsman, Thomas Crapper – hence the reason Scotsmen refer to television as 'The Shitter'.

- The 'coronation chicken' sandwich filling was invented in *Coronation Street*.

- *Countdown* has been running since 1922 – three years before television was invented.

- Right now, somewhere in the world, *Top Gear* is on.

- 'BBC' stands for 'British Broadcasting Co-op', because it used to be a supermarket.

MUSIC

This round won't necessarily mention Three Lions, Oasis, The Beatles or The Houghton Weavers. Even worse than that – it might have questions about classical music. Why that would be of interest to anyone, I do not know. But the following are likely to come up:

- Vivienne Westwood is Tim Westwood's mum.

- Freddie Mercury's real name is Farrokh Saxe-Coburg-Gotha.

- The loudest musical instrument in the orchestra is the Electric Jew's Harp.

- The saxophone solo on 'Baker Street' was played by Anne Robinson.

- Mr T is Jamie T's dad.

- Some square jaw named Bach wrote a few tunes a long, long time ago.

SCIENCE AND NATURE

They're both such important topics that the southerners have to roll 'science' and 'nature' into one round. This is all you need to know:

- Vampire bats are so called because they only drink the blood of vampires.

- On midsummer's day, London is closer to the moon than it is to Leeds.

- The largest glacier in the world tastes of mint.

- Marie Curie invented DNA while experimenting with penicillin in 1984.

- The Earth's core contains two giant pips which will one day grow into two new planets.

This Must Be What It
LOOKS LIKE

Drinking down the Pike View, I hear a lot of talk about fancy inventions from down south. Mostly from Dave The Oracle – because he's the only one who's been there. Now I don't know whether it's the fluorine they put in the air down there or the toothpaste they put in the water, but to give 'em their dues the southerners do have one or two good ideas. Sure, all the best ones – like the spinning jenny, Yorkshire puddings and signing Ivan Klasni on loan – are of course Northern. But I'm a modern man and so I don't mind incorporating a little bit of southern thinking in my everyday life. Let's start with telly.

Flat Screen TV

In his tale 'The Amazing Tablet of Moving Images', Dave The Oracle talks of a shop selling TVs – big ones – that hang on walls and only stick out an inch or two. They're called 'flat screens' apparently and they sound amazing! This is my TV, which takes up half my lounge:

2m

1m

my telly
(to scale)

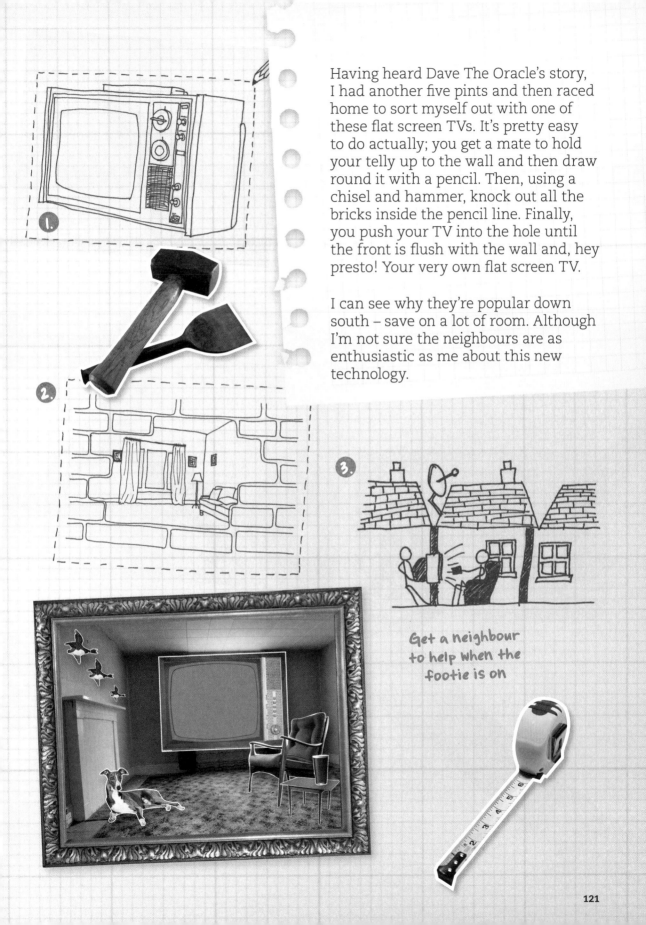

1.

2.

3.

Having heard Dave The Oracle's story, I had another five pints and then raced home to sort myself out with one of these flat screen TVs. It's pretty easy to do actually; you get a mate to hold your telly up to the wall and then draw round it with a pencil. Then, using a chisel and hammer, knock out all the bricks inside the pencil line. Finally, you push your TV into the hole until the front is flush with the wall and, hey presto! Your very own flat screen TV.

I can see why they're popular down south – save on a lot of room. Although I'm not sure the neighbours are as enthusiastic as me about this new technology.

Get a neighbour to help when the footie is on

FUSION RAZOR

It's a fact of life that men have to shave. It's a sadder fact of life that some women have to shave too (*see Prisoner Cell Block H*) – but that's not for now. Down at my barber's there are two types of shave on offer: the cut-throat and the new-fangled safety razor. I don't trust that 'safety' nonsense, so I plump for the cut-throat every time.

It works perfectly. It's fine. It doesn't need changing. But apparently southerners just can't stop tinkering because Dave The Oracle brings news from London of a third type of razor – the fusion razor? It crops up a couple of times in his tale 'The Night I Got Lost In Boots', but you'd be right to wonder just what the hell this fusion razor is.

Well, I'm pretty up on my current affairs and I happen to know that the Iranis keep messing about with fusions so I can only imagine this is their doing. Why on earth you'd want a glow-in-the-dark nuclear razor I've no idea, but I reckon it uses some of the same technology as James Bond's jet-pack in *Thunderball* and must look something like this:

Unlike the flat screen TV, I've got no interest in getting one of these for myself. I'd only drop it and wipe out half of Greater Manchester in a giant mushroom cloud. Mind you, I suppose I could use it in Swindon.

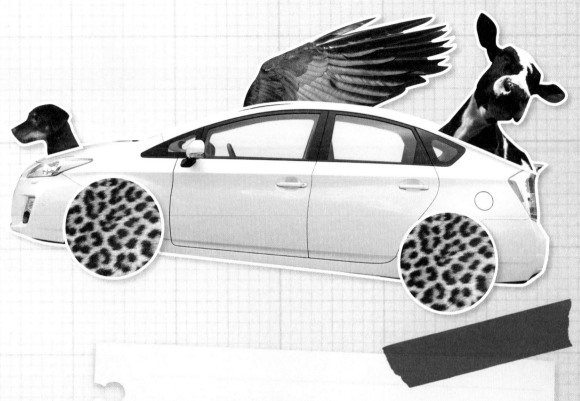

THE HYBRID CAR

....

This is the weirdest of the lot. I realise that cars are getting better and better all the time – I even saw one on the streets of Bolton with a cassette player. But the 'hybrid car' is something else. Dave The Oracle claims to have reversed his truck over one by accident in Ipswich – although he only ever mentioned it once and I think I know why.

It's alive. That's got to be it – that's the only place car makers can go now. The hybrid car is part-machine, part-animal. That's what hybrids are. It looks a bit like a Hillman Super Minx but it doesn't run on petrol, it runs off food scraps. Its tyres are covered in fur, its steering wheel is made of bone, and it doesn't have a radio – it just barks to you. Why anyone would breed such an abomination is beyond me. What sort of person buys this? I'll tell you who – southerners and Jonathan Ross. Weirdos.

Northern Guide To »
LITERATURE

I spent a lot of time researching this topic and eventually I found the information I was looking for: 'literature' means 'books'. Having cleared that up, I set about the very difficult task of picking which works to write about. I say it's a difficult task, not because there are millions of books I could talk about... but because I can't really remember the last time I read a book. Being totally honest, I probably won't even read this one.

6a Our friends

The Ladybird Key Words
Reading Scheme

Peter and Jane Go Fishing
BY LADYBIRD

Now I can't recall the intricacies of this book or any of the twists and turns – but it revolves around a boy, Peter, and his friend... I think her name was Jude. I read it a long time ago so I'm very hazy on the details.

The book explores the relationship between Peter and Janet as they embark on a fishing trip. After many incidents, such as 'seeing a dog' and 'smiling at a man', they find themselves at the river. Once at the river they go fishing and, to their surprise (SPOILER ALERT), they catch a fish. Now I'm probably glossing over the minutiae so, if you want to know more, why not pick up a copy of Peter and Jenny when you're next walking through your local Amazon bookshop.

From what I can remember it was a pretty difficult read. So only pick this one up if you think your reading skills are up to it.

Harry Potter and the Philosopher's Stone

BY J. R. HARTLEY

If you're a fan of Harry Potter, then I should warn you – this book is not as good as the film. They've added a few unnecessary scenes that aren't in the movie and they really slow the book down. Plus the special effects in my head are nowhere near as good as they are on the big screen.

The strangest thing they do in the book is to remove the character Hermyoney and replace her with a girl called Hermione?! That was completely unnecessary.

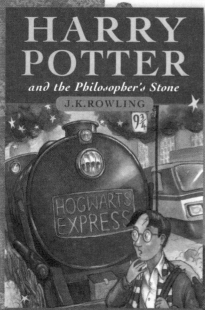

For those of you who have never seen the films, Harry Potter is a wizard who goes to wizard school, meets Hermyoney, an attractive young witch who likes hanging out with him, but he doesn't try to pull her (so he's definitely unsure of his sexuality). He then arselicks the headmaster and groundsman so that they don't mind him playing truant and skipping off into the forest to fiddle about with his wand.

TRIPLE SMARTIES GOLD AWARD WINNER

If I were you I'd save your money and grab a copy of the DVD instead. There's a guy in my pub called Nigel who's selling it for £2. Bargain. Ironically, his business got better after those Knock-off Nigel adverts started running – no such thing as bad publicity (unless you're Gary Glitter or Peter Mandelson).

CHOOSE YOUR OWN ADVENTURE® 2

THE CLASSIC SERIES IS BACK!
CHOOSE FROM 42 POSSIBLE ENDINGS.

JOURNEY UNDER THE SEA

BY R. A. MONTGOMERY

Journey Under the Sea
BY CHOOSE YOUR OWN ADVENTURE

First time I read this I thought it was absolutely brilliant! It was an exciting adventure that seemed never ending. But I picked it up again the other day and all the characters got eaten by a giant fish very early in the story. It didn't feel that short last time I read it.

Determined to review this book, I had another read just now and I must have read it wrong the last time as when I re-read it they avoided the giant fish but instead they end up becoming an attraction at a zoo on Atlantis.

This book is seriously weirding me out. It keeps changing. I think I'm going to burn it.

The Internet
BY STEPHEN FRY

I haven't finished reading this yet, but I plan to get through it by the end of the year. I can't find it in any shops, so you have to read it on a computer. But don't worry – if you don't have one, just give me a shout and I'll print you a copy.

What's The Internet about? Well, at the end of the nineties Stephen Fry started writing everything they knew down on their computer and then connected their computer to everyone else's. Stephen Fry is obviously a big fan of smut, because I've found a lot of it on there, but he does occasionally go too far as there's also some extremely peculiar stuff on there that makes me feel a bit ill. Nevertheless, I am determined to read through all of it.

The book is like the ultimate dictionary; it contains information on everything. I was surprised and honoured to find I was mentioned in there – thanks, Steve! He's obviously a fan. So, you can expect to see me starring in the next series of QI.

I have to say, some of it is amazing, but a lot of it is just terrible. I hope it starts to get better soon as it's getting quite boring at the moment. I'm currently on the section about Rick Astley and I think he's gone into far too much detail.

Paddy's Problem Page

From time to time, everyone needs a shoulder to cry on or a bit of friendly advice. Even Northerners. As such, I'm going to dispense some sage advice to a few people who have written into the local press with their problems.

My husband is an Internet love cheat

DEAR AGONY AUNT, **LIVERPOOL GAZETTE**

I've been married for five years and I have just discovered that my husband is having an affair. Although I've never met my husband in the flesh, he's currently awaiting the death sentence in a Texas prison, our internet marriage vows are still sacred. To my disgust I have since found out he is having the same internet liasons with another 30 different women and a Lebanese goat farmer.

TESSA PHILLIPS, HYDE.

Agony Aunt
Well Tessa, this is not an unusual case for prisoners on death row. Due to their impending doom these D.R. inmates seek solace and warmth from many people over the internet.

Paddy says
Christ almighty Tess, the man's gonna be brown bread in a month! If he wants to spend those last days pumping his fist, while surfing the net, then leave him be. As for the goat farmer, well that's just plain kinky.

He's so untidy!

DEAR AGONY AUNT, **BNP SENTINEL**

My boyfriend and I have been together now for six years and we're planning on getting married in the summer. He's so romantic and gorgeous with his deep blue eyes and blond hair. We're so lucky to have a truly loving relationship. The problem is I'd like him to be a little bit more tidy around the house. It would be wonderful if he'd do the odd bit of housework every now and again.

LISA WALKER, OLDHAM.

Agony Aunt
Untidy you say! How dare he, coming over here taking our jobs!!! We're only an island you know, there's only so many we can take before we sink into the ocean. Those bloody loony lefties, why don't we just let everyone in!!!!

Paddy says
I think you may need to change your newspaper subscription.

star letter

I'm in love with two girls

DEAR AGONY AUNT, **RAZZLE**

I'm 21 and have been seeing my boyfriend for just over a year. But a couple of weeks ago, two new girls started at work. As we are all netball coaches for the Hawaiian tropics female beach volley ball team, you can just imagine how sweaty we all get exercising. After a particular gruelling match, on a beach in Ibiza, we had sand everywhere. Myself and my two new work colleagues, who are also Swedish twins, decided to jump into the sea and wash all that sand off our hot toned bodies. Before I knew it we were heavy petting and got up to all kinds of naughty fun.

Since then I've been ravaged with guilt. I love my boyfriend but now I can't sleep due to the regret I feel for what I've done.

What should I do?

TRIXY BUBBLES,
SENSUALS LAPDANCING BAR, SCUNTHORPE.

Agony Aunt
Well Trixie, that got me all hot and bothered. Why don't you introduce your other half to the twins and you can all have one big love in?

Paddy says
Trixie! Please God tell me you've got all this on camcorder.

I've stopped taking the pill

DEAR AGONY AUNT,
'BOLTON EVENING STANDARD'

Since coming off the pill a few months ago, I've suffered from heavier than normal periods. Is this normal?

JANE SMITH, BOLTON.

Agony Aunt
It certainly is Jane. It's just your body re-adjusting your natural hormone levels and really isn't anything to worry about.

Paddy says
Woah! Okay – I'm done here. Enough problems dealt with for now. Bye!

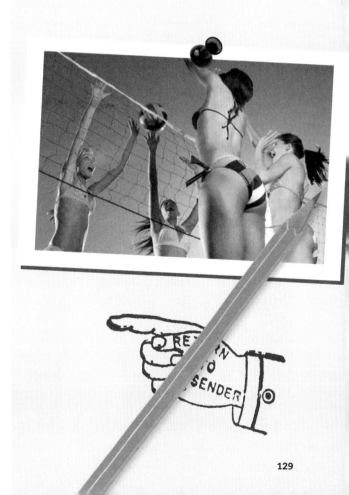

Guide to
LONDON

~ A Brief History Of London ~

London is over 2,000 years old. Back then you could buy a mud hut for as little as £200,000. It seems so little these days. It was at this time Peter Stringfellow opened up his first gentlemen's club.

Life was simple then. There would only be one Starbucks per street and to get around people would walk through the sewers... this would later be known as 'The London Underground'.

After they finished building London it was burned down by Jack the Ripper during the great plague of London. But luckily he was eventually caught by Sherlock Holmes. If you visit London you will see that there are cranes everywhere – that's because they still haven't finished rebuilding it. London will be complete by 2012.

Places Of Interest In London ☞

OLD COMPTON STREET

This is my kind of place. Just a bunch of lads in a pub. No WAGs allowed. And, can I say, they are ever so friendly – they were buying me drinks all night. They must have very understanding girlfriends 'cos not one of them was

phoned or texted at any point in the night to ask why they were not home yet. They had an extremely friendly toilet attendant, although he didn't have any aftershave or moisturiser or anything – very odd. He just had a tub of Vaseline that he said he'd only apply if I went in one of the cubicles with him. Not wanting to waste money I said no and left it at that. Nice fella though.

CAMDEN

This is where every clown in London hangs out. They're all there, walking around with their funny hair, their hilarious clothes and their silly little hats. It's such a laugh! They even have a market at which you can buy all the clown clothes you want. If you're a clown you will LOVE it here. In the true spirit of clowns, they're all very grumpy-looking too – hilarious!

OXFORD STREET

If you ever want to know what fast angry people look like, then this is the perfect place to visit. Want to go shopping? You can't. There's too many fast angry people in the shops. Want to go to the toilet? You can't. They only have one toilet that you have to pay 50p to use, and you have to share it with Ernie the tramp (who apparently used to head a major bank back in the boom days of 2007).

SOHO SQUARE

A heady mixture of money, drug addicts and, at one time, Sven Goran Eriksson.

ABBEY ROAD

If you like traitors, then come here. This is where the best Northern band in the world stabbed their heritage in the back. Liverpool is apparently 'not good enough' for recording music in. So they came down south. Ungrateful little... anyway, there's a zebra crossing here.

EUSTON TRAIN STATION

Better known as 'the way out of London'. In two hours you can be in Manchester. Now that's progress.

Things To Do In London ☞

133

Things To Do In London

The only three things you can do in London are the Millennium Dome, the Millennium Eye and the Millennium Big Ben. The Millennium Eye is part of a fun fair. A fun fair that only has one really slow big wheel – the Millennium Eye. As for the cost? Well, the big wheel in Blackpool costs £2 per family. The Millennium Eye... well, all I'm saying is sell your house before you get in the ticket queue.

And talking of wasting money, why not visit the Millennium Dome? Answer: because no one knows what's in it. Dave The Oracle told me that he went in 2000 and there was a giant's body in it, my cousin went last year and she said there was a ski slope in it, and

the TV said Elton John was in it. I think they're all yanking my chain. Or maybe they just give you some LSD on the way in and everyone just ends up seeing whatever they want to see.

Of course the oldest attraction in London is the Millennium Big Ben. For those of you who have never heard of it – it's the grandfather clock that stands in the middle of London. That's right. A clock. And we've got literally dozens of them up North so it's probably not even worth visiting if you've already seen one.

> **NOTE:** Please make sure all shoelaces are tied, tight and correctly, if visiting London. Any kind of tripping up and falling on the floor could result in a million people walking over you with no regard for your welfare.

SCRATCH 'N' SNIFF

Smells of the North and South

Whether you are a Northerner or a southerner, I want to give you the opportunity to find out a bit more about how the other half lives. And smells.

And here's your chance; I'm getting the printers to add some special 'Scratch 'n' Sniff' patches to these pages so you can sample aromas from different parts of Britain.

So get scratching 'n' get sniffing. I mean scratching and sniffing these pages. I don't want you scratching or sniffing anything else, OK?

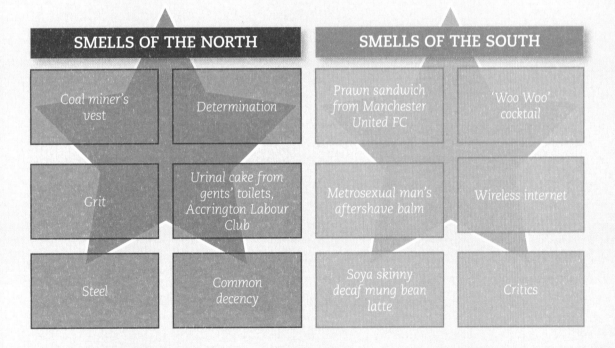

SMELLS OF THE NORTH		SMELLS OF THE SOUTH	
Coal miner's vest	Determination	Prawn sandwich from Manchester United FC	'Woo Woo' cocktail
Grit	Urinal cake from gents' toilets, Accrington Labour Club	Metrosexual man's aftershave balm	Wireless internet
Steel	Common decency	Soya skinny decaf mung bean latte	Critics

NOTE FROM PRINTERS:
Due to the credit crunch, we have been unable to afford the scratch 'n' sniff patches requested by Mr McGuinness. As a result, none of the scratch 'n' sniff panels work. Well, I suppose, except for the last one.

THE McGUINNESS BOOK OF NORTHERN RECORDS

Over the last few years I have been collecting what I believe to be the most important records in the history of the North. Here, for your good selves, are the edited highlights:

RECORD: Fastest 100m

RESULT: 24.3 seconds

RECORD HOLDER: Mick Wentworth

DESCRIPTION: Only 15 seconds off the world record! So that's very close. Although subsequent attempts have been made, Mick Wentworth hasn't been beaten in thirty-two years. In 1992 Roger Wilmslow ran 100m in 10 seconds but it was later revealed that he'd taken a short cut.

RECORD: Longest Fart

RESULT: 1 minute 24 seconds

RECORD HOLDER: Mick Wentworth

DESCRIPTION: This record-breaking attempt was accidentally witnessed by Norris McWhirter when awarding the fastest 100m record to Mick Wentworth (see above). Mick started his acceptance speech with the classic mantra 'Better out than in', which later became the town slogan for Thirsk.

RECORD: Longest Rant

RESULT: A good hour and a half

RECORD HOLDER: Dezzy Lyons

DESCRIPTION: This record was a surprise win by Dezzy, who's normally such a quiet bloke. After being on an all-day bender Dezzy was asked which camp he was in, Team Andre or Team Jordan. The air is reportedly still blue in the Three Crowns.

RECORD: Most Clothes Worn On A Saturday Night In Newcastle

RECORD HOLDER: Tina Rigsby

DESCRIPTION: Tina Rigsby was spotted wearing a coat on 15th January 2003. When asked why she did it, she replied 'Wor idea came to me in a dream'. Newcastle scientists are still trying to work out if there is any benefit to wearing a coat over your boob tube and hot pants on a cold day. The results are currently inconclusive.

RECORD: Most Hen Night Party Guests In A Limo At Once

RECORD HOLDER: Tracey Warburton's hen night

DESCRIPTION: In the summer of 2008 Newman's Limo Hire of Blackpool, in conjunction with Tracey 'Baps' Warburton, managed to squeeze 48 of her hen night guests into the back of one of Newman's stretch limos. The record still stands although an audacious attempt to break it was made earlier this year by Kerry Katona. Unfortunately she was 47 girls shy.

But you have got to take your hat off to the man. After all that, he was still behind the wheel of his HGV the next morning.

RECORD: Most Units Of Drink Consumed In A Single Night

RECORD HOLDER: Rick 'Moobs' Harris

DESCRIPTION: This hasn't been officially sanctioned, but my mate Tez reckons he was there to witness it. Harris started early, so he began drinking at work. Twenty pints later he was looking ropey so Tez fed him some water from a bottle he found. Honest to God, he didn't know it was vodka and lemonade. Then he was sick. Then he drank a yard of ale to win a bet. Then he was sick. So he was given another glass of water. Honest to God, they didn't know there was vodka ice cubes in there. Then he was sick. Then they called last orders so he was given one for the road. Then he had a brief coma. Then he got a cab home. All in all, 70 units downed.

RECORD: Most Cash Borrowed

RESULT: £243,251.72

RECORD HOLDER: 'Tighter than cramp' Terry

DESCRIPTION: This record is not for one single borrowing occasion, but is a build-up of thousands of tiny money-lending requests. TTC Terry accumulated his staggering wealth through various ploys, such as forgetting his wallet, needing some cash for the bus home, and stealing tips in restaurants when everyone else was getting their coats and needing a few quid for the lecky.

RECORD: Biggest Collection Of Road Signs

RESULT: 127

RECORD HOLDER: Jimmy Benson

DESCRIPTION: Jimmy has been collecting street furniture since he started at Sheffield University last year. He has everything from 'Danger: Incomplete Bridge' to the somewhat rare 'Please Refrain From Stealing Our Road Signs'. When asked where he gets most of his signs, he told me, 'I can't remember – they just seem to appear in my house in the morning'. Jimmy's favourite sign is the 'Uneven Camber Ahead'. As a result of his collection, Jimmy is hugely popular among his academic contemporaries. I applaud his dedication. Well done, Jimmy!

RECORD: Greatest Number Of Road Accidents

RECORD HOLDER: The Roads Around Sheffield University

DESCRIPTION: Many believe the reason this area is an accident hotspot is due to the terrible lack of visible signage. Personally, I think it's criminal that the government aren't putting up enough signs around potentially deadly roadworks. And when they do put up signs, they're only up for, at most, a day! I mean, what are they thinking? They need to leave them up for much longer than that. Especially around hazards like incomplete bridges. Bloody government!

EMERGENCY RECOVERY SERVICE

Keep these safety instructions on you at all times. If you ever think you might have wandered down into the south by accident, simply follow these steps...

1 Look down and take note of what you're standing on. Is it cobbles? If it is, you're fine – you're still in the North. If it isn't, then move on to step two.

2 You are in the south. DON'T PANIC. Breathe deeply. Call 0161 496 0496 now and we will send an emergency recovery vehicle to come and get you.

3 Do NOT eat or drink the food – it's posh and so might be deadly (although we're not sure 'cos we can't afford to try it). If you are desperately hungry, then our trained staff will do their best to guide you to the nearest chippy.

4 Do NOT, I repeat, do NOT look in an estate agent's window. The shock could be fatal.

5 Do NOT try to make pleasant or friendly conversation with the locals – this will only confuse and anger them.

6 If someone does attempt to speak to you, do NOT call them 'duck', 'pet', 'pal' or 'chuck'. Instead call them 'old bean', 'guv'nor' or 'me ol' treacle'.

7 BE AWARE. Someone may look like they're talking to you – but check their ears first as they are probably talking to someone else through a wireless earpiece. This is witchcraft. KEEP YOUR DISTANCE!

8 Do NOT drink the tea. It's not dangerous, it's just rubbish and tastes like cheap perfume.

9 Between the hours of 5 p.m. and 6 p.m. STAY INSIDE. Rush hour is extremely dangerous. DO use a sturdy doorway or table for shelter. DO NOT use any lifts. If you are caught outside, just stay perfectly still and hope for the best.

10 If help does not arrive, you can find your own way out by doing a pub crawl. If the beer starts to taste worse and worse, then you're heading south – turn around and head the other way. If you find yourself drinking whisky, then you've gone too far. That's Scotland.

FOUND YOURSELF IN THE SOUTH? CALL 0161 496 0496 FOR EMERGENCY RESPONSE

By keeping calm and following these instructions, disaster can be averted.

PETITION LETTERS

Now it is a well-known fact that down in that London, the people in power don't really care or know much about us outsiders (or, as they refer to us, 'the Others'). I'm sure that they just think we're not worth bothering about because they assume we're all illiterate and incapable of writing an 'X' on a ballot paper. That is of course totally untrue. At least half the kids in my school could write an 'X' by the age of sixteen.

But it doesn't have to be this way. If we unite and demand that things change, then together we can make it happen. Just like Billie Jean King, 'I have a dream!' Except my dream is that, one day, we will have a real Northerner in the House of Commons. OK, so maybe I'm a hopeless romantic, but I could honestly see that happening before

the end of this third millennium. Until then, however, we're just going to have to find another way to make that lot listen.

So the change starts here. I have drafted up a few petition letters championing Northern concerns which you can copy and send off to the bigwigs in that London. If you're not politically minded – no bother. I've done the thinking for you, so just copy my words out and send them off. If you're not educationally minded (i.e. you can't read or write) – no bother either. I've done the writing for you, so just get a blank bit of paper and trace the letters. Come to think of it, you'll probably need to get someone to read these instructions out to you as well. If all else fails, just rip this page out and pop it straight into a post box – it'll probably get there in the end.

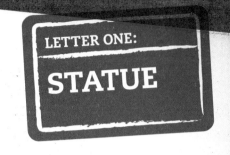

LETTER ONE:

STATUE

PRIME MINISTER
10 Downing Street
That London
The South

Dear Prime Minister,

I am writing to you as a tax-paying member of the British public. (If you happen to check that fact, I should add that, as I've already explained to the Inland Revenue, the postman stole my tax return and cheques 'cos I definitely vaguely remember posting them.) Like everyone who lives on this green and pleasant isle, I deserve to have my say in what you're spending our tax money on.

Instead of chucking all that dosh on a load of nonsense like the Olympics (ten billion quid for a sports day?) or the banks (don't you know, they've already got loads of money? That's what banks do.), you should spend it on things that will make a proper difference.

Here in the North, we are very proud of our cultural heritage; our region gave this great country Alan Bennett, Sir Ian McKellen and Black Lace. As such, I would like to see statues erected in all Northern towns of their most famous cultural icons. To get the ball rolling, I'd like to suggest, for Warrington, a Pete Postlethwaite statue; in Sheffield, a brass representation of Def Leppard, and in Bolton I think you should put up a marble sculpture of, let's say, the hilarious and world-renowned comedian Paddy McGuinness... on a stallion.

If funds are running low, though, make sure you start with the Bolton one first.

Yours sincerely,

(Insert Name Here)

(NOTE: Do not write 'Insert Name Here', just write your name here. NOTE: Not 'Your Name', I mean whatever your actual name is, like, for example 'Wayne Rooney'. But, you know, only if your name is Wayne Rooney. If not, just put your actual name down).)

Prime Minister
10 Downing Street
That London
The South

Dear Prime Minister,

It is my belief that every person in this great country of ours should be equal, regardless of whether they live in the North, South, Left or Right of Great Britain.

That said, there is some stuff from the south-right which we don't want to have equal amounts of up here – you can keep your croissants, your skinny vanilla lattes and your aftershave balm. But when it comes to the important things in life, such as transport, education and ale, then we deserve better.

I see no reason why we should have inferior road surfaces to those in that London. Now I'm not asking you to pave our streets in gold like yours, but we have a right to the best-quality, pot-hole-free streets that money can buy. In this day and age, anything less than the best just isn't good enough.

For this reason, I demand that the government immediately brings our Northern streets up to date by cobbling the lot of them. And while you're at it, make sure you put a telephone wire under the cobbles. We might not be ready for this here internet in every town just yet, but there's no harm in doing a bit of future-proofing.

Yours sincerely,

INSERT NAME HERE

LETTER TWO:

STREETS

Mrs Victoria Beckham
Beckingham Palace
That London
Or maybe America or even Italy

In fact let me start again:

Mrs Victoria Beckham
Wherever the best shopping is
Somewhere

Dear Mrs Beckham,

Before I get to the reason for me sending you this letter, I thought I might just tell you a little bit about the area I come from – the North. That's right, it's that place your husband David used to drive to every day from Hertfordshire when he worked for that shouty Scotsman.

I think you'd really like it here – it's got the best bits of all your favourite cities in the world. It's got the celebrity scene of London, the beautiful climate of Madrid, the fashion buzz of Milan, and the glamour of Los Angeles.

Yes, you'd love it up here. That's the reason I'm writing this letter – I think you and your family should move to the North of Britain. I have no agenda here, I just want you lot to be happy and I think you could be happiest here, living amongst us friendly Northerners.

If you're up for it, I'll sort you out some house viewings in a nice Northern location, like Bolton, and what's more, I'll even fix up a job for your husband at the local football club, now's Megson has gone.

To be frank, even if you don't want to move here, I still think you should encourage your husband to take a job at the Bolton Wanderers.

Yours sincerely,

Insert Name Here

MIDDLESBROUGH

HISTORY

This North-East town located in the Tee valley dates back to medieval times when it was known as 'Mydilsburgh'. As you can see from that spelling, education wasn't so hot back then. During this era, the town is thought to have been populated by Vikings who spent most of their time getting drunk, chasing women and fighting each other. Yes, it was totally unrecognisable compared to the Middlesbrough we know so well.

But it was the Industrial Revolution that transformed Middlesbrough from a tranquil, picturesque riverside hamlet into what it is today. The docks were completed in 1862 and 'Boro quickly became an industrial powerhouse. The then Prime Minister William Gladstone visited the town during this period and declared:

'This remarkable place, the youngest child of England's enterprise, is an infant, but if an infant, an infant Hercules. What do you mean you don't understand? It's an analogy, yeah? I'm saying you're a little town but you will grow up to be great, you get me now? GOD! OK, forget the Hercules stuff. I'll start again. Middlesbrough is a little town at the moment but one day you will be much bigger. If anyone ever uses this quote, I hope to God they stop at the word "Hercules".'

William Gladstone, 1862

NORTH

SCOTLAND

Middlesbrough

WALES

OTHER LESS
IMPORTANT PLACES
(I.E. THE SOUTH)

Middlesbrough has one major claim to fame; it was the first major British town to be bombed during the Second World War. The Luftwaffe bestowed this honour in 1940 and it is commemorated on the signs that greet you as you enter the town boundaries:

'**Middlesbrough:** *say what you want about us, but at least Hitler thought we were worth a bomb.*'

ATTRACTIONS

• **MIDDLESBROUGH INSTITUTE OF MODERN ART** Opened in 2007, MIMA is a 'contemporary' art gallery. You know what that means, don't you? That's right. Not so much your paintings, more your messy beds, your pictures made of dung, and your weird home movies. This place has apparently showcased work by the likes of Eduardo Paolozzi and Elisabeth Frink. While some would say that their work just looks like a load of bollocks, I personally think that Paolozzi's stuff offers a wonderful juxtaposition of bewilderment and illumination while Frink's work is simultaneously inhibiting and enlightening.

• **CAPTAIN COOK'S BIRTHPLACE** Located in Stewart Park, this public museum is a tribute to a genuinely extraordinary man. This legendary naval officer discovered Australia and Hawaii, but he is perhaps most famous for having a big white beard and inventing fish fingers. Wait a minute, I think I'm mixing him up with Captain Birdseye. Or are they the same person? If you go to the museum, please let me know if I'm right about the fish fingers. ≫→

- **THE BIG WHEEL** Middlesbrough's Big Wheel is a fantastic alternative to the London Eye. But only if you live in Middlesbrough, you're scared of heights up to 135 metres, but OK with heights of 40 metres, you're not bothered about nice views, and you enjoy anticlimaxes. You can opt for a bog-standard normal ride – or why not push the boat out and pay for a VIP capsule with champagne? Some 40 metres in the air, sipping champagne, taking in the panoramic views of 'Boro you'll get a taste of what life must be like for Jay-Z and Beyonce.

- **ROY CHUBBY BROWN** For those of you not aware of his work, Roy is a legend of the stand-up comedy scene. Truth be told, I find some of his stuff a bit blue. It would be nice if he downgraded some of his C-words to F-bombs, and his F-bombs to s-h-1-ts. Not only a top comedian, Roy holds the Guinness world record for making the word 'FLAPS' funny. He's done more for flying helmets and goggles than Biggles ever did.

FAMOUS SMOGGIES

- **PAUL DANIELS** What a showman! What an entertainer! What a purveyor of the dark arts! Born in Middlesbrough, Paul Daniels regularly entertained millions of viewers with his magic tricks and memorable catchphrases such as 'You'll like this, not a lot, but you'll like it', 'Now that's magic!' and 'That David Blaine's a right dickhead'. In his time, Paul Daniels has even made elephants disappear. But the trick he'll best be remembered for is somehow convincing the lovely Debbie McGee to marry him. I tell you, that's not a trick that's a bloody miracle.

JOURNEY SOUTH When you think of *X-Factor* success stories, the first act you probably think of is Leona Lewis. Then you think of Alexandra Burke. Then Shayne Ward, then Joe McElderry, G4, Steve Brookstein, Andy Abraham, Tabby, Same Difference, Leon Jackson, JLS, Jedward, Ray Quinn and Chico. But the next act you think of (if you can think as far as this) is probably Journey South. And they're from Middlesbrough. So there you go.

PUBLIC HOLIDAYS

• **PRETEND DAY** This Middlesbrough tradition occurs sporadically and takes place whenever a visiting foreign (usually Brazilian) football star is in town for contract talks. The people of Middlesbrough all put their lights on to make it look sunny, flock to the beach in their swimming costumes to make it look tropical, and everyone smiles for twenty-four hours. Then the football club drive the likes of Alves, Juninho and Emerson round the town with the in-car heating turned up to full. Once the contract is signed, 'Pretend Day' is over and 'Reality Day' begins.

• **REALITY DAY** The reverse of above.

LOCAL TRIVIA

• The Middlesbrough Transporter Bridge is regularly voted the town's 'Prettiest Ugly Landmark'.

• Middlesbrough residents are often called Teessiders and they invented the Tee-shirt as a short-sleeved item of clothing to keep people warm in sub-zero temperatures while out clubbing.

• The most famous people who've never been to Middlesbrough are Elvis Presley and Magic Johnson.

• If you call a Smoggy a Geordie or a Mackem, you will regret it.

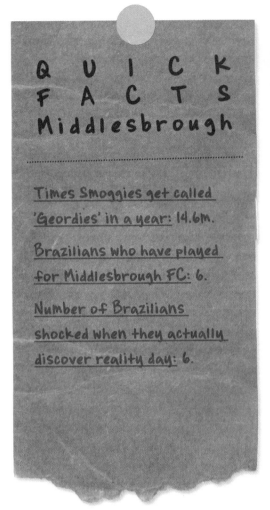

QUICK FACTS
Middlesbrough

Times Smoggies get called 'Geordies' in a year: 14.6m.

Brazilians who have played for Middlesbrough FC: 6.

Number of Brazilians shocked when they actually discover reality day: 6.

HARROGATE

HISTORY

Evidence of settlers in Harrogate dates back as far as the 10th century, but it was in the late 1800s that the town really put itself on the map as a popular destination for English nobility.

As a result, Harrogate has become so posh now, it can no longer be classed as a Northern town, even though geographically it's still in Yorkshire.

During a visit to Harrogate, Oscar Wilde reportedly said:

> 'I have nothing to declare, except that Harrogate contains the most uptight, poncy, stiff-upper-lipped twats I have ever had the misfortune to meet. I can't wait to get back to Chelsea where the people are much more salt-of-the-earth.'
>
> Oscar Wilde, 1882

These days, Harrogate operates much like West Berlin used to within East Germany. A twelve-foot-high concrete wall has been built around Harrogate's boundaries to prevent unauthorised Northerners from entering the town. The only Northerners who are authorised to enter are the servants who work for the Harrogatians and even they are only allowed in between 7 a.m. and dusk. If they stay beyond dusk, they are humanely thrashed.

NORTH

SCOTLAND

Harrogate

WALES

OTHER LESS
IMPORTANT PLACES
(IE. THE SOUTH)

ATTRACTIONS

• **HARROGATE SPAR** Harrogate is what's known as a 'Spar' town, which means people from all over Britain flock to it because they believe it can bring them health benefits. And it's all true because behind the counter next to the camera films, they do stock an excellent range of medicinal products including paracetamol, throat lozenges and Rennies. Visitors also come to the Harrogate Spar for its mineral water along with its energy drinks and alco-pops.

"Citizens of this town are too busy drinking high tea and hunting pheasants to be bothered with fame"

• **HARROGATE INTERNATIONAL CENTRE** Who will ever forget what happened here in 1982? Eurovision descended on North Yorkshire and Jan Leeming hosted the singing competition from the HIC. The artists that performed here on 24th April 1982 went on to dominate the world. There was the Swedish band Chips with their anthem 'Dag Efter Dag', the Finnish musician Kojo's nuclear warning song 'Nuku Pommiin' and, of course, Portugal's Doce with the catchy 'Bem Bom'.

• **TK MAXX** When it comes to shopping in Harrogate, this is pretty much the only shop that normal folk can afford to buy anything from. And even then you'll probably only have enough to buy socks or a belt.

FAMOUS PEOPLE WHO WERE BORN IN HARROGATE

To be honest, asking around Harrogate, they don't really have many famous sons or daughters. Some of the *Emmerdale* cast are rumoured to live here, but not anyone famous. The citizens of this town are too busy drinking high tea and hunting pheasants to be bothered with fame.

FAMOUS PEOPLE WHO TEMPORARILY WORKED IN HARROGATE

This is a much richer vein.

• JOHN CRAVEN

John Craven OBE began his career as a junior reporter on the *Harrogate Advertiser*. But he quickly moved to the *Yorkshire Post*.

• JAN LEEMING

In 1982, Jan presented a singing competition in the town. She left the next day though.

• KOJO

The pioneering anti-nuclear Finnish musician Kojo visited Harrogate in the early eighties. He also left the next day.

"Hasselhoff has performed twelve times, but is yet to inspire the demolition of the Harrogate Wall"

PUBLIC HOLIDAYS

• SERVANTS' DAY

Once every four years the servants of Harrogate are honoured on this special day. Their reward for four years' hard work takes the form of a forty-five-minute paid lunch break, during which they celebrate by eating the leftover caviar and quails' eggs from their employees' silver breakfast platters.

• MONEY BONFIRE NIGHT

On Tuesday evenings the people of Harrogate head to Valley Gardens for a special bonfire. Entry is £1,000 per person in cash but rather than handing it over at the turnstile, the Harrogatians place the notes on to a bonfire. At 8 p.m. sharp the bonfire is lit and the onlookers politely applaud while their servants stare at their shoes, trying not to cry at the injustice of it all.

LOCAL TRIVIA

• A typical family meal in Harrogate involves eight courses, sixteen types of knife and fork, twelve varieties of spoon, and the services of three butlers per diner.

• Harrogate Spar is slightly smaller than Bath Spar due to the latter's sizeable freezer section.

• Having brought down the Berlin Wall with his message of freedom through soft rock, David Hasselhoff has performed in Harrogate twelve times, but is yet to inspire the demolition of the Harrogate Wall.

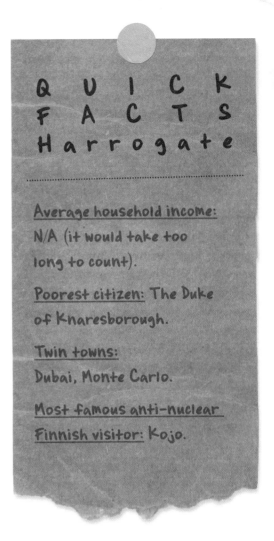

QUICK FACTS Harrogate

Average household income: N/A (it would take too long to count).

Poorest citizen: The Duke of Knaresborough.

Twin towns: Dubai, Monte Carlo.

Most famous anti-nuclear Finnish visitor: Kojo.

HULL

HISTORY

Located on the north bank of the Humber Estuary, Hull was granted its royal charter in 1299. Coincidentally, £12.99 is the average house price in Hull in 2010. The town's full name is 'Kingston Upon Hull'. Being in the North, and quite rightly so, the locals thought that name sounded a bit too 'fancy', so they just shortened it to 'Hull'.

In a well-documented meeting between Samuel Johnson and James Boswell in 1777, Dr Johnson memorably referenced Hull in one of his most famous quotes:

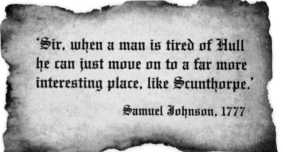

'Sir, when a man is tired of Hull he can just move on to a far more interesting place, like Scunthorpe.'

Samuel Johnson, 1777

During the Second World War, Hull saw some of the most severe bombing raids the UK has ever seen – 95% of the city's houses were damaged or destroyed. When Winston Churchill subsequently visited the town to inspect the damage, he exclaimed, 'Oh, what a terrible scene. Never have I witnessed such a desolate and ugly sight'. The Mayor replied, 'No. The bombed bit's over there'.

NOTABLE HULLENSIANS
(PEOPLE WHAT COME FROM HULL)

· **NORMAN COOK (aka FATBOY SLIM)**
'Tank fly, boss walk, jam nitty-gritty you're listening to the boy from the big bad city. This is jam hot. This is jaaam hot.'

If it wasn't for Norman Cook, you'd never have heard these words (well, at least not in that order), because he was the brains behind 'Dub Be Good To Me'. Now, I'm no dance music expert (I prefer a bit of Christian rock), but in my view Fatboy Slim is behind some of the best ever songs in the house, garage or conservatory music genres. Norman/Fatboy has also been in top notch pop acts such as The Housemartins, Beats International and, of course, who can forget Yum Yum Head Food. He's a musical legend and he's from Hull. I still don't know what a 'Tank fly' is though. Or a 'boss walk'?

· **JOHN PRESCOTT** Hull lad John Prescott is one of the greatest heavyweight fighters ever to emerge from this great isle. His reactions are so fast, he could knock you out cold as quickly as it takes a farmer to throw an egg. But like all great fighters, he's had his problems over the years, like bulimia (the problem being he forgot to throw up), infidelity (the problem being he got found out), and owning two Jaguar cars (the problem being taxpayers actually owned them). Those who accuse him of being a typical Hullensian man – a cheating, overweight, incomprehensible, violent, croquet-playing cretin – are completely wrong. Hullensian men don't play croquet.

· **DEAN WINDASS** I thought about including another famous Hullensian here, William Wilberforce. He was the man who forever changed Britain when he pioneered the abolition of slavery in the 1800s. But while that's all very clever and selfless of him, it's not exactly a local boy scoring the winning goal in the Championship play-offs to get Hull into the Premier League for the first time ever, is it? And that's why Dean Windass is getting a mention here. ≫→

*"Deano's in his early forties and Gandhi was seventy before he got **properly warmed up**"*

The lad got Hull into the top flight with a cracking volley at Wembley and, for that reason, he'll forever be loved by the people of Hull. Yes, he's not made any notable contributions to the advancement of human rights in the UK and yes, he's not been responsible for 200 years of social advancement. But give him a chance – Deano's in his early forties and Gandhi was seventy before he got properly warmed up.

PS Speculation that Dean Windass is the fattest premier league player of all time is totally unfounded, he's just big boned.

LANDMARKS

• **KING GEORGE DOCK** Hull's King George Dock provides an excellent way to leave Hull by sea, with ferries travelling to several interesting destinations including Rotterdam and Zeebrugge.

• **HUMBER BRIDGE** The nearby Humber Bridge provides an excellent way to leave Hull by road, with good road links to several interesting locations such as Liverpool, Manchester and Bolton.

• **HULL PARAGON INTERCHANGE** This transport hub provides an excellent way to leave Hull by rail or by bus, including main line services to several interesting cities, if you count London as interesting?

• **HUMBERSIDE AIRPORT** Though it is twenty miles from Hull, this airport nevertheless provides an excellent way to leave Hull by air, with destinations including several interesting countries like The Netherlands and Scotland. The duty-free shop does a great deal on ciggies.

• **HULL BIG SCREEN** Now everyone jokes about Hull being out-of-touch just because it's stuck out in the middle of nowhere. But that's just an unfair stereotype. For example, Hull's got telly. Well, one big one; in 2004 the people of Hull clubbed together and bought themselves one massive TV which is proudly displayed in the city centre. There are currently plans to buy a second TV after Saturday night riots broke out over whether to watch *Strictly Come Dancing* or *X Factor*. Plans for Sky+ are just pipe dreams at the minute, but Hull City Council is working hard for Virgin Freeview.

PUBLIC HOLIDAYS

• **ANNUAL AWAY DAY** Once a year, the citizens of Hull are allowed to leave the city and see what life is like in the rest of the UK. But before they're let out, they have to promise that even once they realise how nice the rest of the country is, they still have to return to Hull by midnight. If this rule is broken, residents must sit in a dark room, for two hours, repeating the words: London is shit, Hull is tops.

LOCAL TRIVIA

• Rod Hull didn't come from Hull, but Emu was made there.

• The local paper, the *Hull Daily Mail*, is a lot like the national newspaper the *Daily Mail*, except it focuses on local matters and is much less xenophobic.

• Hull is the only UK city with its own independent telephone network (Kingston Communications); in the coming decades, plans are in place to introduce text messaging services but let's walk before we run.

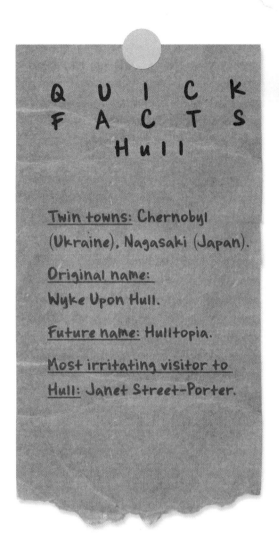

QUICK FACTS
Hull

Twin towns: Chernobyl (Ukraine), Nagasaki (Japan).

Original name: Wyke Upon Hull.

Future name: Hulltopia.

Most irritating visitor to Hull: Janet Street-Porter.

LANCASTER

HISTORY

Lancaster stands on the River Lune and was first discovered by Romans in boats ages ago. But no one was really very interested in it until the mid-1400s when a fight broke out between some people from a house in Lancaster and some people from a house in York.

York is miles away from Lancaster and they didn't have cars back then, so I've no idea how this fight kicked off, but it lasted for ages and came to be known as 'The Wars of the Roses'. Now I'm no historian, but I'll bet both sides liked the big purple ones with a hazelnut in the middle and probably left those manky strawberry ones in the gold wrappers. That always causes arguments in my house particularly around Christmas. Anyway, after some tit-for-tat wrapper tossing, the Lancaster lot eventually won and it all settled down again until about 1600.

"Because of the 1612 'trouble', **Which?** *magazine isn't stocked anywhere in Lancaster."*

By that time, the whole of Lancashire had become overrun with witches. They were everywhere mixing potions, casting spells and not brushing their teeth like nobody's business until, in

NORTH

SCOTLAND

Lancaster

WALES

OTHER LESS IMPORTANT PLACES

(IE. THE SOUTH)

1612, the good folk of Lancaster decided they'd had enough and complained to the king, James I.

He then came over, caught twelve witches in a witch-net, confiscated their Quidditch brooms, and locked them up in Lancaster Castle. The Pendle Witch Trials took place the following day and then they were all hanged. To this day, hanging a witch is considered good luck in Lancaster. For that very reason, you will never see Mystic Meg, Russell Grant, Derek Acorah or Lady Sovereign there.

"Lancaster is also home to the world's blindest policeman – those lights were definitely not red. **TIT!!!**"

ATTRACTIONS

• **LANCASTER CASTLE** Don't go here. For a start, this is the place where all those witches were hung back in 1612 and they're always on the lookout for more so, if you're a woman, steer clear (especially if you like wearing hats). And if you're a bloke, steer even clearer because half of the castle is a working men's prison so there's a very real chance of being mistaken for a jailbreaker and getting banged up for a ten-stretch. On the plus side, it does have a nice gift shop.

• **THE M6** Not only is the M6 the oldest motorway in Britain, it's also the longest! And what's more, it passes just to the right of Lancaster. If you come off at junction 33 you can take the A6 all the way up through Lancaster before joining the M6 again at junction 34. But be warned, the northbound entry slip road here is very short so you'll need to put your foot down. (Lancaster is also home to the world's blindest policeman – those lights were definitely not red. TIT!!!) ⟫→

• **BAILRIGG** Just south of the city centre, nestled beautifully between the M6 and the A6, is Bailrigg the Lancaster University campus. There's lots to see and do on-site: the Peter Scott gallery houses the university's international art collection, and for poetry fans there's the Ruskin Library which has the world's largest collection of manuscripts, photos and paintings by the great John Ruskin. But, more importantly, there are eight colleges on campus each of which has its own bar. That's eight bars full of young, impressionable students selling really, really cheap booze.

> "WWII *fighter plane*
> **the Lancaster Bomber**
> *didn't drop a single bomb*
> *on Lancaster.*"

FAMOUS LANCASTRIANS

• **ELIZABETH DEVICE** She might not actually have come from Lancaster, but Elizabeth Device certainly ended up there swinging from a rope having been tried as a witch. Although she did apparently have a wonky eye. Not a hanging offence as such, but makes you think.

• **ERIC MORECAMBE** Wasn't strictly born in Lancaster – he was actually born in Morecambe. But Lancaster's favourite son was a true entertainer. No one made wobbling glasses and slapping faces funnier than Eric.

• **JIM BOWEN** OK, so Jim wasn't born here either, but he did live in Lancaster for a bit. And what a legend. Sunday isn't Sunday without a bit of Bully! Well, it is, but... you know what I mean.

PUBLIC HOLIDAYS

• **HANGING DAY** Once a year, on the anniversary of the Pendle Witch Trials, the inhabitants of Lancaster hang one-eyed puppets from their bedroom windows.

• **ANNUAL HOTPOT PARTY** Nowhere is the traditional Lancashire hotpot more celebrated than in Lancaster. It's a simple but tasty combination of onions, potatoes and meat left all day to bake in a warm oven. And on this particular day, the townsfolk all gather together to make one huge hotpot which they then share out equally. It's a real party atmosphere, it's fun for all the family and the meat is exquisite – not sure what it is, but it tastes like chicken. Anyhow, the party apparently takes place the day after Hanging Day.

PS People with glass eyes (Peter Falk) are not welcome.

LOCAL TRIVIA

• Because of the 1612 'trouble', *Which?* magazine isn't stocked anywhere in Lancaster.

• Despite its name, the famous WWII fighter plane the Lancaster Bomber didn't drop a single bomb on Lancaster.

• HRH The Queen also holds the title 'Duke of Lancaster', which presumably means everyone in Lancaster thinks she's a man.

• Lancaster is the only city in Britain whose name contains all five vowels.

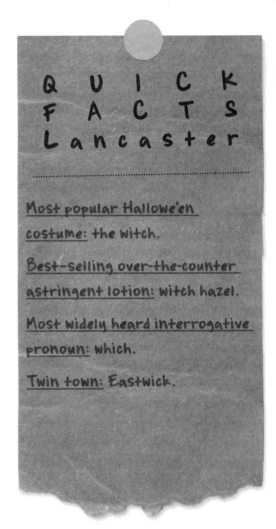

QUICK FACTS Lancaster

Most popular Hallowe'en costume: the witch.

Best-selling over-the-counter astringent lotion: witch hazel.

Most widely heard interrogative pronoun: which.

Twin town: Eastwick.

VERY LOCAL Free Ads FROM THE NORTH

FOR SALE

GARY GLITTER back catalogue. Not many requests for this in my current job. Tom's mobile disco, kids parties a speciality, Clitheroe.

RICE One portion would have been enough but the wife insisted on two. She doesn't want to eat it, but doesn't want to bin it either. Will swap for two poppadoms, or one with chutney. Craig, Blackburn.

WEDDING DRESS Worn once. Also, wedding cake (uneaten), 12 carnation buttonholes (wilting), 120 portions of steak and chips (on the turn). Assorted items of ripped men's clothing. £10.00 the lot. Susan. Ps. F*ck you, Billy.

SANDWICHES Also cheese and onion pasties, steak bakes, sausage rolls, tins of drink, doughnuts, scones, iced buns, occasionally a bit of fruit – all sorts on offer actually. We are a shop after all. Greggs, Bolton.

WANTED

CHANGE Anyone got change for a fiver? No pennies or two pound coins please. Contact Baz on the fruity in The King's Arms.

NEW BOYFRIEND Not fussy. So long as they actually make it up the aisle and aren't called Billy. Thanks, Susan.

BATTERIES Does anyone know where they are in Boots? I'm next to the Tena Ladies. Pete.

YALE LOCK KEYS Anyone know where I left them? I've locked myself out again. Dunc at number 32.

APOLOGY I want an apology. You bloody well know why, you w*nker. Susan.

GENERAL SERVICES

LAMB OR CHICKEN Which do you want for your tea, Steven? I'm off to Lidl – according to Sandra, it looks like they're out of chicken. Love you. Linda.

CORGI REGISTERED But now what do I do with it? Gareth.

TV HIRE Don't all come at once though – I've only got one. Tony's TV Warehouse.

LOST AND FOUND

OSSETT I'm lost in Ossett. Is it the B6128 or the B6129 that gets us to the M1? Thanks, Pat.

MY WATCH Lost it somewhere in the town centre. You know – it's the square one with the brown strap. Anyone seen it? Ta, Paul.

THE M1. I've found it. Thanks anyway. Pat.

KIDS' CORNER

HAPPY 21st BIRTHDAY Nanna! Have a great day, love, from all your grandkids. Liverpool xxx.

ANNOUN-CEMENTS

For the attention of Toby. Now you're old enough to deal with it we have some news for you: you're adopted.

OSAMA BIN LADEN

Well, the world and his dog have been looking for old Sammy bin Laden for the best part of a decade now without any luck. Even the American army with its heat-seeking missiles, Hubble telescopes and George Formby grills hasn't been able to find the tricky little bugger.

It reminds me a bit of when my mate Toddy fell off the face of the earth. One Saturday night he borrowed forty quid off me and promised he'd give it back in the pub the next day – but he never showed up. I was livid. After all, we're not talking £15, or even £18 here. We're talking forty quid! Serious money.

"We're talking forty quid! Serious money."

Like the USA with Sammy bin Laden, I wanted to hunt Toddy down quickly to complete our unfinished business. I started my manhunt by going round his house, but his mum said he'd gone out. Then I went to our local, but no one had seen him there either. So then I called round at my pal Johnny's, he's got one of those chipped cable boxes, and sure enough Toddy was there.

So, my advice to Mr Obama and his soldiers would be to first check at Mrs bin Laden's house. I bet they haven't even bothered going round there yet – or, if they have, they probably haven't checked the wardrobes or the loft. But if he's not there, find out from them Taliban fellas which local he drinks in. I'm no expert on the pubs in Tora Bora but they must have

> "Find out from them Taliban fellas which local he drinks in."

fellas Al Jazeera and Al Qaeda (isn't it an amazing coincidence that all his pals are called 'Al'?), so their gaffs would probably be a good first port of call. And I bet you anything, old Sammy'll be round one of their houses watching the free porn on their chipped cable boxes.

In fact, I'm so confident that they'll track him down using my methods, I'll give the Americans forty quid out of my own money if they don't find him. Well, technically, I'll just transfer Toddy's £40 debt from me to them because he still hasn't paid me. Just threaten him with the Guacamole Bay – that should shake it out of him.

a Wetherspoon's, and Wetherspoon's are always full of dubious characters with beards. However, if Sammy's not there supping on a pint of mild, then it's time for Plan C.

Plan C is basically call round Sammy's pals' houses (or caves). From what I've heard, he's very friendly with them

FAMINE

Back in the eighties, Sir Bob Geldof was responsible for trying to solve the world's problems (famine), but was also guilty of creating some new world problems (Peaches, Trixie, Lala and Po). However, Band Aid, Live Aid and Band Aid 2 (the Lisa Stansfield/Kylie/ Technotronic version) did not solve the problem of famine.

From what I've heard, there are still people in some parts of the world who can't afford to eat every day. I can only assume that they must be trying to buy their weekly shop in Waitrose's. You'd have to be Roman bloody Abramovich to shop in there. So perhaps the first course of action should be to start

and he's only got one sofa and two kitchen drawers – there must be hundreds around the world. Then what they should do is take all those coppers down the fish & chip shop and spend them on scraps and battered sausages. It's tasty and it's good for you.

> *"Each sachet counts as one of your five a day."*

It's also worth visiting service stations and cafés and taking the free ketchup, salt and salad cream sachets when the staff aren't looking. I'd imagine that each sachet counts as one of your five a day, so fill your boots and you'll be full up in no time.

Martin's clever thinking got him through that week – and the next, after he lost yet another Giro down the bookies. So people of the world – take note. Don't thank me – that's HRH's job. And if you're reading this, Ma'am, you have to admit that 'Sir Paddy' has a certain ring to it.

shopping in Netto's instead. Now, obviously it's not as simple as that. I know full well that not everyone has a Netto's nearby. For example, Keswick doesn't have a Netto's within eighteen miles of it – so the people of Keswick must know exactly what it's like for those less fortunate around the globe. But those third-world countries that do have Netto's should make good use of them.

For those countries that don't have a Netto's, I hold up my pal Martin as a role model. Back in '94, he blew his entire Giro in Ladbroke's betting on Ayrton Senna to win the Italian Grand Prix. Long story short, Martin lost the bet. This meant that he had to survive for a week without any money at all. And I wasn't about to put my hand in my pocket for him because looking after yourself is an important life skill that I wanted Martin to learn.

And those less fortunate countries could learn a thing or two from Martin's innovative approach to food shortages; to start off, they should check down the back of sofas and in their kitchen drawers for spare coppers. He found £1.62 that way

GLOBAL WARMING

This one's a biggie. Big-brained boffins in laboratories all over the world have done experiments with test tubes, drawn graphs on squared paper, and done calculations with slide rules to prove that the Earth is getting hotter. On average, they reckon, temperatures around the globe will rise by 2 degrees over the next century if we carry on like we are at the moment.

That might not sound like much, but let's just take a step back; Northern folk – particularly the Scots and the

Geordies – already find the UK's balmy climate almost unbearably hot. They literally can't take any more clothes off without being naked. If temperatures increase by anything like 2 degrees centigrade, there's a very real possibility that this lot will melt. And from what I've gathered, if Northerners melt into the North Sea they'll cause the sea levels to rise, drowning fish and flooding the ice cubes in the Arctic.

Now, global warming is all caused by something called the greenhouse effect. So my first suggestion is that people stop building greenhouses immediately. It's obviously not helping and I'd go so far as to say that anyone who already owns a greenhouse should knock it down. For the good of the planet, people in glass houses should

start throwing stones. The left-over glass can simply be burnt on a bonfire – although you might need a few tyres on there first to get the thing going. I recommend cross radials, they really keep the heat.

The second big cause of global warming seems to be the highly dangerous gases emitted by car exhausts. My solution to this is twofold: firstly, everyone needs to tie a bit of rag, or an old sock, over the end of their exhaust – that should catch most of it. And secondly, car-makers need to start making the exhaust pipes narrower. I don't know why they haven't thought of that already – but, Mr Ferrari, if you're reading this, a little Testarossa-shaped thank you in racing red wouldn't go amiss.

"You don't ever want to meet a hot Geordie."

OK, those are all good ideas, but I know what you're thinking – smashing up greenhouses and sticking socks over exhausts takes time. What can the people of Britain do right now to combat global

warming? Well here's the answer: leave your fridges open. All of them. Go and do it now. The more fridges we can leave open, the colder this country will get. Move the milk out of the door shelf and stick it at the back – that way it'll stay cold. Everything else will be fine. It's amazing how doing something small like that can save the planet.

But don't do it because I told you to – do it for the fish. Do it for the polar ice cubes. And do it for us Northerners – because, trust me, you don't ever want to meet a hot Geordie.

ISREAL Vs PALESTINE
(PMcG Solution)

I'm going to be honest and admit that I'm not 100% on the ins and outs of the old Issy/Pally conflict. I know I occasionally wear glasses, but that doesn't make me Alfred bloody Einstein.

But I'll do my best to explain to you what I do know about it. Basically, Palestine had some land and then Israel moved in and started taking over the place. It's a bit like when I shared my house with my mate John – he'd leave crap all over the living room and there'd be nowhere to sit. Ungrateful. Anyhow, what made the whole conflict worse was when he started to hog the telly zapper. Now I could have lost control and dropped some f-bombs or exploded in a fit of rage, but instead I took him down the pub where we discussed the issue over

a beer and some peanuts. Then we popped into Laser Quest to settle it once and for all.

John, who used to be part-time TA, thrashed me and so I let it go. (Although I did get a hit ratio of 87% which means I was technically the better shot.) So what I'm saying is this: Benjamin Netton-Yahoo (could someone check my spelling before this goes to print?) and Matt-Mood Abba (check that one too, ta) should follow my example and settle their conflicts over a few pints, some peanuts and a game of Laser Quest. Or if they think Laser Quest is a bit too violent, they could just go bowling instead (there's usually one next door to Laser Quests). So that's Israel and Palestine sorted. I don't know what all the fuss was about.

And by the way, if anyone from Question Time is reading this and wants me to help sort out national issues, then I'm available for most of the year (apart from Panto season, when The Trotters are playing or when Columbo is on).

> "We popped into Laser Quest to settle it."

To paddy, thanks for teaching me all my fighting skills. Top one.

Your mate

Sly Stone

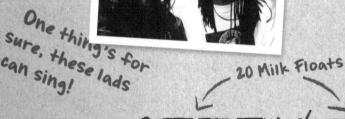

Paul Gascoigne
ENGLAND

Jimmy Phillips
BOLTON

Mrs Kylie McGuinness

Mrs Debbie Gibson-McGuinness

Mrs Tiffany McGuinness

~~Mrs Sonia McGuinness~~

Mrs Linda Lusardi-McGuinness

If I can't have you, Sam, no other man can either x x x

Paddy Knievel

Paddy Kneivel attempts the Milkfloat/needle Leap of DOOM!

One thing's for sure, these lads can sing!

20 Milk Floats

Skip full of syringes

Paddy's SCRAPBOOK

BOLTON BETAMAX RENTALS
MEMBERSHIP CARD

NAME: MR P. McGUINNESS

DATE OF BIRTH: 1st January 1950

RENT: ACTION, COMEDY, FAMILY, BLUE, VERY BLUE

RENT: U's, PG's, 15's, 18's & UNDER COUNTER STUFF

RENT: BETAMAX, VHS & LASERDISC

Dream Jobs:

1 Hitman
2 Steven Seagal's stunt-double
3 Centre forward for Bolton Wanderers
4 Oil Boy on Baywatch
5 Dough-mixer machine cleaner at Warburtons

Heroes:
- Big Daddy
- John McGinley
- Tiswas

Shopping List

~~Nunchuks~~
~~Katana blade~~
~~Ninja throwing stars~~
~~BB gun~~
Conan the Barbarian calendar

Inventions & Ideas:

- Hover-tank
- X-ray pants
- Invisible gloves
- TV show called **TAKE ME OUT**
- Battered chips

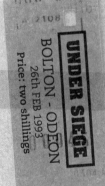

UNDER SIEGE
BOLTON - ODEON
26th FEB 1993
Price: two shillings

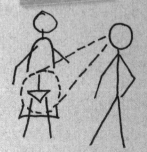

Whether you're a southern lady who wants to blend in up North or a Northern lady who wants to make the best of herself, old Gok McGuinness is here to help you with some GM makeover tips.

BEFORE

FACE - Whoops! This fake tan is wrong with a capital 'W', sister! And where did you learn to do make-up? In the dark?

TOP - No, no, no, girlfriend! Real ladies should not dress like this!

SKIRT - Um, hello?! 'Good taste' has just left the building!

WRISTS - Knock knock! Who's there? Accessories, sweetheart! Where are the accessories?

HIGH HEELS - Darling, what kind of a message are these white monstrosities sending out?

170

★ AFTER ★

FACE – That's more like it! A healthy glow to set off her natural-looking complexion.

TOP – Sweetie, that look is so-oo 2010. Now you look like a lady.

WKD BOTTLE – This accessory sends out a powerful message, girlfriend! 'I'm having fun, and I'm probably up for it.'

SKIRT – Three words for you, sister: classy, classy, classy, we're seeing more of that chassis!

BOOTS – Check out these babies. Darling, your feet just got super-sophisticated!

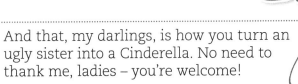

And that, my darlings, is how you turn an ugly sister into a Cinderella. No need to thank me, ladies – you're welcome!

WANTED!

FOR CRIMES AGAINST THE NORTH

KATHRYN (KATE) ADIE

WHILE THE NORTHERN COURT APPROVES OF MS ADIE'S WELL-DOCUMENTED CONDUCT IN THE FACE OF REPEATED DANGER, THERE ARE CERTAIN ASPECTS OF THE NORTHUMBERLAND-BORN LADY'S BEHAVIOUR WHICH CAN NO LONGER BE IGNORED.

'ANY PERSON BORN IN THE NORTH OR RESIDING IN THE NORTH MUST ADHERE STRICTLY TO THE UNWRITTEN NORTHERN CODE (PETER STRINGFELLOW BEING THE EXCEPTION). FAILURE TO BEHAVE IN THE NORTHERN WAY OR ACTING IN A MANNER WHICH MAY BRING THE NORTH'S STEELY NO-NONSENSE REPUTATION INTO DISREPUTE IS A CRIMINAL OFFENCE.'

◄ NORTHERN LAW STATUTE 37c ►

⟫⟫ CRIME 1:
FOREIGN TRAVEL

Travel is not something a Northerner aspires to, and it should be engaged in sparingly. Northern Law Statute 92d clearly states:

'Foreign travel is permissible for the following reasons only – up to a combined total of four days (three nights) in any one calendar year:

i) A football match (UK mainland only)
ii) A funeral (UK mainland only)
iii) A honeymoon (south coast, Midlands caravan park and/or Norfolk Broads only)
iiii) A lads' piss-up

' "Visiting a relative", "Business" and "Just to see if I'd fall off the edge of the world" are not acceptable reasons for travelling south of Chester. Truck drivers are exempt.'

Northern Law Statute 92d

Ms Adie (who has never been a truck driver) is in clear, repeated and televised contravention of this statute; she's not only been abroad, she's been abroad-abroad – to places like Libya, China, The Falklands, the former Yugoslavia and Iraq. This Court neither has extradition agreements in place with those countries nor does this Court really know where any of them are.

➤ CRIME 2:
WRITING AUTOBIOGRAPHIES

While every Northerner leads a life which will be of immediate interest and fascination to anyone who resides south of the border, there is absolutely no need to write a book about it. Let alone four books, all of which are – in one way or another – autobiographical. Writing books is a southern pastime (unless, of course, it's a book specifically about the North and how much better it is than the south) and, as such, falls under the 'Banned Southern Pastimes' addendum to Appendix 6 of the Northern Statutes. It will not be tolerated.

Ms Adie's crimes are heinous. She may think she's safe living in that London, but this Court shall not cease in its quest to see her brought to justice. Don't hand yourself in just yet, Katie, as the Court has yet to decide what sort of punishment would be worse than getting shot at in war zones for twenty years straight. Any constructive advice from Ms Adie would be welcome and may result in a reduced sentence.

➤ CRIME 3:
LEARNING

The Northern Court is a progressive body and realises the value of gaining a solid education and good higher-learning qualifications such as GCSE Welding, NVQ in Slag Heap Management, O-Level Whittling or a BTEC in Smelting.

Kate Adie has, however, attended university – and then obtained a degree, which is big-brained show-offiness of a sort specifically prohibited by Northern Statute 12j. This much learning is far too much for one person and clearly dangerous. For that reason the Court does not advise anyone who spots Ms Adie to approach her. She may lecture you and then demand you sit an exam.

NORTHERN POLICE DEP
CASE FILE

SIGNATURE:

P McGuinness

FILE NO: 44291

FILE NAME: ADIE/K

OFFICER: P.McGUINNESS

WANTED!

FOR CRIMES AGAINST THE NORTH

VICTORIA BECKHAM

WHILE MRS BECKHAM NEITHER CURRENTLY RESIDES IN THE NORTH, NOR WAS SHE BORN HERE, SHE IS STILL WANTED BY THE NORTHERN COURTS FOR CRIMES COMMITTED WITHIN OUR BORDERS DURING THE YEARS 1997 TO 2003.

'ANY PERSON BORN IN THE NORTH OR RESIDING IN THE NORTH MUST ADHERE STRICTLY TO THE UNWRITTEN NORTHERN CODE (PETER STRINGFELLOW BEING THE EXCEPTION). FAILURE TO BEHAVE IN THE NORTHERN WAY OR ACTING IN A MANNER WHICH MAY BRING THE NORTH'S STEELY NO-NONSENSE REPUTATION INTO DISREPUTE IS A CRIMINAL OFFENCE.'

⟨ NORTHERN LAW STATUTE 37c ⟩

⟫ CRIME 1:
ENCOURAGING A MAN TO WEAR A SARONG

While it is not known whether Mrs Beckham was solely responsible for making a man wear a sarong, by merely condoning this action she is party to a serious crime.

'It is a Northern girlfriend's/wife's duty to prevent her boyfriend/husband from leaving the house looking like a tart. Failure to do so is illegal and will not only result in a heavy fine for the female involved, but also a compulsory punishment of severely over-the-top and quite near-to-the-knuckle mocking by the unusually dressed man's pals.'

Northern Law Statute 68d

⟫ CRIME 2:
ENCOURAGING A MAN TO GO TO A FASHION SHOW

The only dating locations that are acceptable for those who reside or have resided in the North are: the football, the 2 for 1 restaurants, the pub, the working men's club, the living room or Blackpool. By having her husband accompany her to one or more fashion show(s), Mrs Beckham is damaging the very foundations upon which the North was built. And the North was 'built' – it wasn't 'designed and stitched'.

➤➤ CRIME 3:
SPICE WORLD

➤➤ CRIME 4:
GIVING UN-NORTHERN NAMES TO HER CHILDREN

Unfortunately, Mrs Beckham has given her children names that are not eligible in the North. 'Brooklyn' is a place; 'Romeo' is off a Leonardo DiCaprio film; 'Cruz' is what you do on a Spanish ferry. Because of her blatant disregard for the Northern way, this Court now has the power to re-name Mrs Beckham's children with names that actually exist in the North. So from now on her sons will be named Compo, Iqbal and Foggy.

Should Mrs Beckham ever step on Northern soil (or cobblestone) again, then she will immediately be arrested and made to pay for the above crimes. There is one caveat; if Mrs Beckham is in the North because her husband has signed for Bolton Wanderers FC, then the Northern Court promises to turn a blind eye to these past misdemeanours. If he signs for Burnley though, the penalties will be doubled.

NORTHERN POLICE DEPT. CASE FILE

SIGNATURE:

P McGuinness

FILE NO: 110485	
FILE NAME: BECKHAM/V	
OFFICER: P.McGUINNESS	
RESULT: CASE CLOSED	

WANTED!

FOR CRIMES AGAINST THE NORTH

GORDON RAMSAY

THE NORTHERN COURT HAD LONG BEEN WORKING UNDER THE MISAPPREHENSION THAT, DUE TO HIS ALOOF AND SELF-SATISFIED DEMEANOUR, MR RAMSAY WAS OF SOUTHERN ORIGIN. HOWEVER, IT HAS RECENTLY COME TO THIS COURT'S ATTENTION THAT HE IS, IN FACT, SCOTTISH. YEP, I WAS AS SURPRISED AS YOU ARE. HIS BIRTHPLACE IS JOHNSTONE, WHICH IS IN RENFREWSHIRE. WHICH IS IN SCOTLAND. WHICH MEANS THAT HE IS COMFORTABLY WITHIN THE JURISDICTION OF THIS COURT AND SHOULD KNOW BETTER THAN TO BEHAVE LIKE A FANCY DAN.

'ANY PERSON BORN IN THE NORTH OR RESIDING IN THE NORTH MUST ADHERE STRICTLY TO THE UNWRITTEN NORTHERN CODE (PETER STRINGFELLOW BEING THE EXCEPTION). FAILURE TO BEHAVE IN THE NORTHERN WAY OR ACTING IN A MANNER WHICH MAY BRING THE NORTH'S STEELY NO-NONSENSE REPUTATION INTO DISREPUTE IS A CRIMINAL OFFENCE.'

⊣ NORTHERN LAW STATUTE 37c ⊢

≫ CRIME 1:
ACCENT FRAUD

From Mr Ramsay's accent, you might think he grew up in Windsor Castle. But he was actually born twelve miles from Glasgow so, by rights, he should sound less like Prince Philip and more like Rab C. Nesbitt. His swearing ratio does give away a few tell-tale signs, but swearing alone won't help. Northern Law Statute 86f states:

'The only circumstances in which it is acceptable for a Northern man to put on a southern accent are:

a) To pretend to bailiffs that he is someone else
b) When talking to Her Majesty the Queen
c) If he finds himself alone on a train full of Millwall supporters.'

Northern Law Statute 86c

≫ CRIME 2:
REPEATED TORSO EXPOSURE

While it is acceptable for a Northern man to expose his torso in some circumstances (e.g. football changing rooms, bare-knuckle boxing, sheep-shearing), Mr Ramsay repeatedly and unnecessarily goes topless. If God had wanted Northern men to expose their chests, he wouldn't have invented string vests.

⤜ CRIME 3:
BEING A MAN WHILE COOKING AND SHOWING OFF ABOUT IT

The Northern Court in no way condones sexual discrimination and believes that, in this age of equality, there is nothing wrong with men doing a bit of cooking. This is not a crime. However, if you go around showing off and writing books about it, that is a crime. Mr Ramsay is welcome to do whatever he likes behind closed doors, but there is no need to bang on about it in public. We can all do sausage and egg on toast, but we don't all walk round bragging about it.

⤜ CRIME 4:
GRIEVOUS CUISINE BETRAYAL

As a man of Scottish birth, Mr Ramsay must, by Northern Law, deep-fry at least 50% of his food. However, our Food Inspector made undercover visits to his restaurants on several occasions and made three important findings:

a) There wasn't so much as a bog-standard deep-fried pizza on the menu

b) Unlike in Scottish restaurants, in Mr Ramsay's establishments a tenner will definitely not cover your meal

c) Mr Ramsay's waiters are very quick runners and possess excellent rugby-tackling skills

While Mr Ramsay's crimes would normally result in an automatic Northern life sentence, we are prepared to negotiate the terms if he hands himself in. More specifically, we are willing to drop all of the charges against Mr Ramsay if he waives the £236.20 debt which our Food Inspector now owes him.

NORTHERN POLICE DEP
CASE FILE

SIGNATURE:

P McGuinness

FILE NO: 080486

FILE NAME: RAMSAY/G

OFFICER: P.McGUINNESS

RESULT: CASE CLOSED

WANTED!

FOR CRIMES AGAINST THE NORTH

CRISTIANO RONALDO

Mr Ronaldo is wanted for crimes committed against the North in the Old Trafford and Alderley Edge regions of Lancashire between the years 2003 and 2009.

➤ CRIME 1:
DRESSING LIKE A PROPER TART

See exhibit A. There is no excuse for this.

➤ CRIME 2:
BEING A MAN WHILE SIMULTANEOUSLY WEARING AN EARRING

The only jewellery permitted for Northern males is as follows: sovereign rings, Mum/Dad rings, and 21st or 18th birthday necklaces. No other jewellery will be tolerated!

➤ CRIME 3:
OILING HIMSELF UP LIKE A BLOODY CHIPPENDALE

See exhibit B. Northern men are not permitted to wear any kind of sun protection. If Mother Nature had intended Northern man to sunbathe, she would have given the North sunshine.

➤ CRIME 4:
HAVING A RIGHT FANCY HAIRCUT

The only hairstyles that are legal for a male in the North are:

1) Short back and sides
2) Number two all over
3) Tramlines (special occasions)

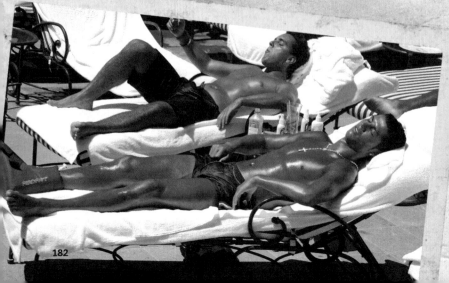

⟫ CRIME 5:
ROLLING AROUND ON THE FLOOR LIKE A LITTLE GIRL

When a Northern man is physically injured, he must on no account let on that he is feeling any pain. The crime of 'Showing Pain' results in extensive verbal abuse from fellow Northerners. GET UP, MICK, IT'S ONLY A BLOODY SCRATCH, YOU SOFT B***ARD!!!! But the more heinous crime of 'Simulating or Exaggerating Pain' is an automatic one-way ticket to the south.

In 2009, Mr Ronaldo evaded Northern border control and fled to Spain to avoid punishment for dozens of crimes committed during his time in the North.

The North is currently seeking Mr Ronaldo's extradition from Spain but is, to be honest, struggling to cobble together the £80 million release fee requested by his employers.

If you see Mr Ronaldo, do NOT approach him. Not because he's dangerous, but because he's likely to go down like a sack of spuds if you get within five foot of him.

NORTHERN POLICE DEPT.
CASE FILE

SIGNATURE:

PMcGuinness

FILE NO: 230184

FILE NAME: RONALDO/C

OFFICER: P.McGUINNESS

RESULT: CASE CLOSED

WANTED!

FOR CRIMES AGAINST THE NORTH

GORDON SUMNER

WHILE THIS SUSPECT WAS BORN 'GORDON SUMNER', HE MAY ALSO BE OPERATING UNDER THE CRIMINAL ALIAS 'STING' TO TRY AND OUTWIT THE NORTHERN AUTHORITIES (WHICH HE HAS SUCCESSFULLY DONE THUS FAR). A NATIVE OF NEWCASTLE UPON TYNE, MR SUMNER LEFT THE NORTH IN 1977 BUT HAS BEEN GUILTY OF DISREGARDING THE NORTHERN CODE ON SEVERAL OCCASIONS.

'ANY PERSON BORN IN THE NORTH OR RESIDING IN THE NORTH MUST ADHERE STRICTLY TO THE UNWRITTEN NORTHERN CODE (PETER STRINGFELLOW BEING THE EXCEPTION). FAILURE TO BEHAVE IN THE NORTHERN WAY OR ACTING IN A MANNER WHICH MAY BRING THE NORTH'S STEELY NO-NONSENSE REPUTATION INTO DISREPUTE IS A CRIMINAL OFFENCE.'

NORTHERN LAW STATUTE 37c

▶▶ CRIME 1:
TALKING ABOUT 'SLAP AND TICKLE' IN PUBLIC

There are only two places it is acceptable to talk about 'How's Your Father?' and that's with male friends in the confines of a Working Men's Club or with yourself in your own mind. Discussion of 'bedroom gymnastics' is not appropriate in any other circumstances for fear of looking like a soppy pervert.

▶▶ CRIME 2:
STITCHING UP OTHER NORTHERN MEN BY GIVING THEIR WOMEN UNREALISTIC EXPECTATIONS

Nookie sessions of eight hours are not only forbidden in the North, for fear of Northern women ending up thinking this is something they are all entitled to, it is also the stuff of complete and utter nonsense. The maximum legal duration of a 'Horizontal Jog' in the North is four to five minutes weekdays, a good ten minutes on a weekend. Anything above and beyond this is the work of machines and Peter Stringfellow.

CRIME 3:
SINGING IN A NON-NATIVE ACCENT

As Mr Sumner was born in Newcastle Upon Tyne, he is required to sing in a Geordie accent like Jimmy Nail. However, audio evidence discovered in HMV has proved that, at several points during his career, Mr Sumner has sounded a bit Jamaican (see Exhibit A: 'Walking On The Moon' and Exhibit B: 'Message In A Bottle'). On other occasions he just sounds like a wrong 'un. If found guilty of this offence, Mr Sumner will be forced to do 200 hours' community service learning how to sing Geordie with Lindisfarne.

CRIME 4:
HAVING AN INELIGIBLE NORTHERN NICKNAME

The nickname 'Sting' breaches the official guidelines for Northern Nicknames. The only acceptable forms of nickname are:

a) Adding 'o' or 'ey' or 'ster' to the end of the first syllable of a person's forename

b) Adding 'o' or 'ey' or 'ster' to the end of the first syllable of a person's surname

This means that Mr Sumner's only legal Northern nicknames would be Gordo, Gordey, Gordster, Sumno, Sumney or Sumster.

CRIME 5:
PLAYING A LUTE

Guitars, bass guitars and drums are the only acceptable instruments for a Northern male to play (piano is also acceptable if you are Sir Paul McCartney). Lutes may only be played in the North by Southern-born pretentious cream cakes and should be confined to the 1800s.

NORTHERN POLICE DEP
CASE FILE

SIGNATURE:

P.McGuinness

FILE NO: 86766

FILE NAME: SUMNER/G

OFFICER: P.McGUINNESS

RESULT: CASE CLOSED

WANTED!

FOR CRIMES AGAINST THE NORTH

LIAM GALLAGHER

WHILE MR GALLAGHER LEFT THE NORTH IN THE MID-1990S TO BECOME A NORTHERN AMBASSADOR IN LONDON, HE MUST STILL BE HELD TO ACCOUNT FOR THE GRIEVOUS BETRAYALS OF HIS NORTHERN ROOTS. HIS CRIMES WERE MAINLY COMMITTED IN THE LA-DEE-DA LOOK-AT-ME AREA OF PRIMROSE HILL, LONDON, BETWEEN THE YEARS 1994 AND 2009.

'ANY PERSON BORN IN THE NORTH OR RESIDING IN THE NORTH MUST ADHERE STRICTLY TO THE UNWRITTEN NORTHERN CODE (PETER STRINGFELLOW BEING THE EXCEPTION). FAILURE TO BEHAVE IN THE NORTHERN WAY OR ACTING IN A MANNER WHICH MAY BRING THE NORTH'S STEELY NO-NONSENSE REPUTATION INTO DISREPUTE IS A CRIMINAL OFFENCE.'

⊰ NORTHERN LAW STATUTE 37c ⊱

➤ CRIME 1:
SETTING UP A FASHION LABEL WHILST BEING A NORTHERN MAN

According to Northern Law, the only people permitted to set up fashion labels are fancy posh ladies and Frenchmen. Mr Gallagher's Pretty Green fashion label contravenes these Northern regulations and so, should any items from his clothing range be found in the North, they will immediately be incinerated to protect the Northerness of our men.

➤ CRIME 2:
BEING 'INTERESTED' IN FASHION

This crime goes hand in hand with Crime 1. The extent to which a Northern man is legally allowed to be interested in fashion is detailed in Northern Law Statute 72d:

'A Northern Man will accept whatever his wife/ girlfriend/mother or any other female relative gives to him. End of. Any further expression of opinion or interest in clothing is un-Northern. Replica football shirts are the only exception.'

➤➤ CRIME 3:
SPORTING UN-SPORTING SPORTSWEAR

Shorts and ladies tights. There isn't a country in the world where that is legal, not even the Philippines or France. This crime is exacerbated by Mr Gallagher's proximity to a tiny un-Northern dog.

➤➤ CRIME 4:
HAVING A LADY'S HAIRCUT

Long or feathered hair is only permissible in ladies, hippies and Lemmy from Motorhead. Further charges may be made against Mr Gallagher if, on further investigation, it is revealed that he is in possession of hair straighteners or any kind of Class A banned hair 'products' (which includes every hair washing/styling item except Morrisons Value Shampoo and Brylcream).

While Mr Gallagher is wanted for the above crimes, it is believed that the real mastermind behind these offences is his accomplice, a Ms Nicole Appleton. While she is not Northern herself, she can still be found guilty of the crime of Aiding and Abetting De-Northernisation.

Should Mr Gallagher give himself up and testify against Ms Appleton, he would simultaneously have any potential sentence reduced (for aiding the Northern Law authorities to make an arrest) and would also have any potential sentence increased (for being a dirty grass, which is against Northern Law).

NORTHERN POLICE DEPT.
CASE FILE

SIGNATURE:	FILE NO: 98451
	FILE NAME: GALLAGHER/L
P McGuiness	OFFICER: P.McGUINNESS
	RESULT: CASE CLOSED

189

NORTHERN
CHAT-UP LINES

How To Treat A Lady

Well, you've got this far in the book so I'm going to treat you. That's right, I'm going to give you some of Magic McGuinness's love tips. If you're a girl – stop reading now! This page contains information that would blow your pretty mind.

So, it's just us lads now? Good. So after reading this, you boys will know all my dating secrets (or 'strategies'). You will become hot property. A pulling professional. A love magnet. A sexual predator.

You'll be interested to know that these techniques get different results in different parts of the country, so I will be showing you how to change each 'strategy' to suit your environment.

STRATEGY ONE:

Determination

When you try to bag yourself a beauty, you have to give it your all. I like to follow this rule:

'If at first you don't succeed? Try, try, try, try, try, try, try and try again. Then beg. Then get angry. Then start shouting. Then apologise. Then cry.'

You'll be amazed at how much female attention this gets you. Our readers in Burnley needn't have read this step, as there's no such thing as crying there.

STRATEGY TWO:
Chat-Up Lines

Chat-up lines are the starter to love's main course. If you're really lucky, the lady might let you skip the main course and go straight to the sweet stuff. Be careful with these lines. They're powerful beasts. And with great power comes great responsibility.

'If I could rearrange the alphabet, I'd put Y-O-U and M-E together. What I'm saying is, come on, it's been three months and I'm desperate.'

(NOTE: This cannot be used in Swindon or Norwich as it relies heavily on the ability to spell. For similar reasons, the line can't be used on Peaches Geldof.)

'Are you an ornithologist? 'Cos if you show me a couple of tits, I'll show you a happy little pecker.'

(NOTE: On saying the word pecker, you must thrust your hips backwards and forwards – at roughly the same rate as humming bird's wings.)

'Hey, let's make like the Highways Association trying to reduce speed-related accidents on a particular road, and hump.'

(NOTE: Try to remember the word, hump, for this one, as the words, chicane, bollard, adverse camber and speed camera don't have the same sexual connotation.)

'Have you got a hammer and nails? 'Cos I've got wood.'

(NOTE: A double-handed pointing down to the crotch usually alleviates any doubt in the lady's mind as to what you're on about.)

'D'you like crisps? Can I feel yer naughty pillows?'

(NOTE: The first bit is optional, it's only small talk. Oxford and Cambridge readers might like to replace. 'Can I feel yer naughty pillows?' with the question 'Do you have any male friends?'

'That's a nice dress. Can I feel yer naughty pillows?'

(NOTE: I'm just showing off the versatility of that line.)

(NOTE: Doesn't work in Liverpool. It only works if they wear knickers.)

'They call me "name tag" – because I'm gonna be spending a lot of time in your knickers.'

'My car's battery's flat. Want to jump me?'

(NOTE: And if they don't like You've Been Framed, then they're probably not worth it.)

'Do you like You've Been Framed? Because if you show me a couple of boobs, I'll show you a cock up.'

'Are you any good at impressions? Because I want you to do me.'

(NOTE: Not for use in London as there are no such things as semi-detached houses. There are just mansions and palaces.)

'Are you looking to buy a house? Well I've got a semi for you.'

(NOTE: I am, of course, referring to my willy. Readers in Essex may need to make this very clear to the girl, perhaps by adding the words 'with my willy' at the end.)

'I may be an intelligent, inspiring, generous person, but don't worry if you're not. I'm sure a part of me will rub off on you later.'

(NOTE: Don't go thinking that this isn't factually accurate as, in London, there is a straight man that is in fact a beautician. Beggar's belief – I know!)

'I'm a beautician. Can I touch you up?'

STRATEGY THREE:
⬧ First Date ⬧

So she's putty in your hands. But where to go on a first date? Don't worry; lovemaster McGuinness can help you there. Here are some suggestions for locations, which will make that first date end with a bang (and then some).

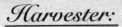

Harvester:

The money you save on the free salad bar can be spent treating your lady to a more premium quality pint of bitter. Women like a man who's good with money.

Fun Fair:

What says 'I love you' more than winning her a flammable Homer Simpson toy on the Hook-a-Duck? This appeals to her more primeval side as it shows you're a good hunter-gatherer, provided you have a bamboo stick with a hook on the end and that your prey has a metal loop sticking out of its head.

Bowling:

Show her how brilliant you are by taking the game really seriously and rubbing it in her face when you give her a hiding on the skittles. Then why not follow it up by thrashing her at a game of pool. Remember to make a very flattering Sid James 'PHWOOAR' noise every time she bends over to take a shot. She can't fail to be impressed by those skills.

Ballet:

Let her see that you are a connoisseur of the arts. But make sure you bugger around for a bit before leaving the house – do anything you can to miss the first hour or so. Failing that, purchase some of those novelty glasses with the eyes painted on the front and have a kip during the so-called performance.

Night In:

Invite her over to your house and watch a romantic film like *The Terminator*. It's so beautiful when Reese and Sarah Connor finally get together. It's a better love story than any of those olden-day films that Jane Austen is in.

Footie:

Take advantage of the fact that it's early days, so she won't kick up a fuss if you take her to a match. This way, you don't miss the game, she thinks it's a date, and you start the relationship as you mean to continue. It's win-win.

I can promise you that each of these strategies have been fully thought through by me and double checked by Dave The Oracle, so they can't fail*.

*Should these strategies fail, you will **NOT** be refunded for these pages and you will be relocated to London.

How-To GUIDES...

HOW TO... WEAR A FLAT CAP

The humble flat cap is an essential part of any Yorkshireman's wardrobe. At a glance it might look like a simple tweed head-warmer, but beware – it can be deceptively difficult to wear correctly if you are a first-timer. So, if you're thinking about wearing one – or just need a short refresher course – take a moment to read my easy three-step how-to guide. Otherwise, you might end up looking a right tit.

PEAK ALIGNMENT: As with all Yorkshire clothing conundrums, the first port of call should always be *Last of the Summer Wine* – more specifically, Cleggy.

The key point to notice here is the forward-facing direction of the peak. Don't worry about the slight sideways slant of the cap – that's something the more experienced wearer can experiment with. Just focus on getting the thing on the right way around.

The gentleman on the left is wearing his flat cap correctly. The gentleman on the right most definitely isn't. Just remember this simple rhyme – peak to the front, don't look like a c***(use your imagination here).

HAND TO HEAD: Once you're confident you can identify the front of a flat cap from the back, it's time to bring the hat to your head (never attempt the reverse). Holding the flat cap firmly with your left hand at the back and right hand at the front, raise the hat to the head in one fluid motion. Remove hands, shake out any residual tension, and have a cup of tea.

CHOICE OF FABRIC: Flat caps can be worn in a wide variety of colours and fabrics – as long as they're all brown tweed. Everything else is unacceptable.

Now you're a competent flat-cap wearer, see page 200 to learn how to smoke a pipe.

HOW TO... RACE PIGEONS

When you think of Northern sports, you immediately think of pigeon racing, rugby league and badger baiting. Sadly, one of those sports is now illegal up here (rugby league was outlawed for being too soft). But pigeon racing remains the most noble, graceful and adrenaline-packed sport of them all.

You may not realise it, but racing pigeons is not as easy as racing humans. You can't just line them up in a row and expect them to waddle down a set of painted running track lanes like they do in athletics. I learned that the hard way. It was rubbish. Plus, the starting gun scares them all off.

But I have picked the brains of some of the greatest pigeon racers in Bolton (well, mainly Dave The Oracle) and here are the most important things to remember if you want to have a go at pigeon racing yourself.

GET YOURSELF A PIGEON:
Firstly, it's probably best to outline two places you should NOT get your pigeons from: the butcher's because those pigeons are racing nowhere; and the steps of Bolton town hall because they are wild maverick birds, and not professional racing ones.

No, the best place to get your pigeon is from a breeder. Breeders have the best pigeons – if you think about it in human terms, they're essentially getting Usain Bolt and Linford Christie to mate so that a super-racing bird-child is produced.

TRAIN YOUR PIGEON:
Every pigeon-fancier has their own techniques for training their birds, but they usually involve building a pigeon loft and letting the racers get used to their environment before gradually moving them farther from home and allowing them to fly back. While pigeons have incredible homing instincts, you might not want to rely on instincts alone. That's why I'd advise enrolling your pigeon on to a geography degree course. That way, they can use a mix of instinct and just looking at geographical landmarks.

PIGEON-FRIENDLY VEHICLE:
As well as a pigeon loft, you'll also need to invest in a vehicle so you can transport your pigeon to the location of the race. You can get specialist vehicles for this, but Dave The Oracle assures me that if you just clean out your glove compartment, there's usually enough space to put a pigeon in there. You will need to drill a couple of airholes so the pigeon can breathe, though it's best to do that before you put the pigeon in. Again, learned that the hard way. And it cost me a few quid at the car wash to get it all rinsed out.

LET YOUR PIGEON GO AND HOPE FOR THE BEST:
Once you release your bird and the race has begun, there's not a lot you can do really. Step one is to find your own way home. This one's not so easy for me – once took me twelve days to get home from Blackburn to Bolton. Then it's a waiting game. In an ideal world, a few days later your pigeon will return to your pigeon loft and win the race. However, there are plenty of potential hazards out there – such as larger birds of prey, light aircraft and Ken Livingstone.

Simple, isn't it? As long as you stick to these rules, you can't go far wrong. And hopefully, you won't end up making the same mistakes I did and buy a racing pigeon from a guy in the pub who you've never seen before. Turned out he'd stolen it from Chester Zoo. And it was a penguin. Bloody flightless! Took the poor little bastard five months to waddle home from Doncaster.

HOW TO... MAKE A SCALLOP BUTTY

In case I haven't already made this totally clear, Northerners love their food. I'm not talking about your posh restaurant guinea pig's eyebrows served on a bed of thinly sliced, cherrywood-smoked hedgehog flaps, I'm talking about proper food: hotpots, pies, Pot Noodles – and the king of them all: the scallop butty.

But before I get started on how to rustle up God's dinner, let's get one thing straight. A scallop butty does not, in any way, ever contain anything related to one of these:

Dave The Oracle claims people do actually eat these down south – and not just to win bets. I suspect he's pulling my leg because I don't care how hungry you are, there's no way THAT constitutes food. And even if you did, in some moment of madness, try to put it in between two slices of bread and wolf it down, that shell would reap havoc with your fillings.

No, a scallop butty contains these:

THAT is a scallop. Now I've cleared that up, let's get down to business.

THE INGREDIENTS All you need to make the perfect scallop butty are two slices of bread (white extra thick) butter (best), some ketchup (any sort so long as it's red), a potato (any), a knife (bloody sharp), some batter (see your local Chippy), a deep fat fryer and some deep fat.

Bread, butter and ketchup come from the corner shop. If you need help finding those, then it's a wonder you're even here reading this book. A potato is a bit more exotic, but don't panic because it's just the thing chips are made out of. Cut it out, take it to the shop and keep looking until you find something that matches. (Note: if you find something that looks like this but is bigger (or smaller) than the photo, that's fine – it's still a potato.)

If it's very hard and breaks your teeth upon chewing, it's a piece of coal.

A knife comes from the cutlery drawer. Batter I'm not too sure about – I don't really know where that comes from. But they have it down the Chippy, so perhaps you can buy some from there. When it comes to the deep fat fryer, just look around the house – you'll probably have two or three dotted about the place. Kitchen's a good place to start looking. Or, if you're like me, you've probably got one by the sofa in the living room too. And finally, deep fat is the stuff that powers deep fat fryers. It's usually in there already so I shouldn't worry too much about that one.

THE PREPARATION Using the knife, slice the potato into thick crisps. Using the knife again, spread butter on to both bits of bread (one side only if you're watching your weight). Then (and this bit's important), still using the knife, make sure the seal on the ketchup is broken.

Dip the thick slices of potato into the batter and then drop them into the deep fat fryer. If they don't immediately start sizzling, turn the deep fat fryer on and try again. Once they've been in there for a bit, take them out again – although don't use your hands because boiling fat smarts. Hey presto! Through the magic of deep fat, your potato has turned into scallops.

Pile the scallops up on top of one of the slices of bread. Squirt ketchup all over until you can't see the scallops any more and then put the other slice of bread on top. And that, my friend, is it. Now comes the fun part...

THE FUN PART: If you're going to eat the butty in the house, clingfilm the furniture and lay a groundsheet down first because ketchup's a bugger to get off. Then just sit back, put the footie on and prepare to sample a little slice of heaven... well, several slices of deep-fried heaven smothered in ketchup and sandwiched between two bits of bread. The North was built on food like this.

And there you have it – the best butty in the world. If you're an expert-level chef, you could consider adding bacon to the equation. Or,

if it's a meal you're after rather than just a snack, why not add a third slice of bread in the middle and triple-stack it? Or, if you're cooking to impress a lady, try using salad cream instead of ketchup – sauce sophistication. And if anyone finds out where batter comes from, can you let me know? Ta.

PS Salt and vinegar can be applied within reason.

HOW TO... SURVIVE THE COLD

Let's face facts: it can get a bit chilly up here in the North. However, true Northerners are built to deal with it in a way that southerners just aren't. Take that old-Etonian southern tart Bear Grylls for example. He might have survived some pretty inhospitable conditions in his time and been in the SAS, but dress him in a short-sleeved Ben Sherman shirt of a December night and stick him out on the town in Doncaster and he wouldn't last two minutes. So, for those southerners who'd like to learn how to deal with the cold better, I will now impart some advice, techniques and tips which'll help explain how us Northerners do it so well.

DEFINING 'COLD' Firstly, we must answer the question 'what is cold?' By Northern standards, anything above 0 degrees is classed as 'Christ, it's warm'. Anything between 0 and -5 is 'warm', -6 to -15 is classed as 'nippy', and then anything below that is officially 'cold'. That's all the categories there are. Technically, you can define anything under -25 degrees as 'Fleeing', but that's really just a subset of 'cold'. So recalibrate your thinking and it'll help a lot.

SELECTING SURVIVAL ATTIRE: CHRIST, IT'S WARM (0 DEGREES OR ABOVE) If it's 0 degrees or above, just remember to wear loose, breathable clothing so you don't get too hot or dehydrate too quickly. Light cotton or bri-nylon clothes and breathable footwear will help with this.

WARM WEATHER (0 to -5 DEGREES) Moving from 'Christ, it's warm' to 'warm', you might want to consider a lightweight covering-up top for the gents, or a midrift-warming belt for the ladies.

NIPPY WEATHER (-6 TO -15 DEGREES) Now, you'll need to wrap up a bit to deal with those subzero 'nippy' temperatures. A short-sleeved shirt and jeans for men should do the job.

And for the ladies, a short skirt and vest top should give sufficient protection from the more moderate elements. Though ladies, as temperatures head closer to -15, underwear may also be advisable.

FLEEING WEATHER (BELOW -25 DEGREES) In Fleeing weather, you'll need to pile on the layers.

Fingerless gloves are now required to keep your hands warm while still being able to pick up your pint without fear of slippage. Obviously, a scarf on a Northern man is still a no-no – we're not foreign footballers, are we? But make sure you keep that scarf on if you're of the female persuasion. We're not barbarians.

POKER FACE: However you're feeling, however freezing you may be, the key is not to show it. That would be a sign of weakness and, of course, us Northerners do not have any weaknesses. So whether you're male or female, it's time to MAN UP. Restrain the shivering. Stick your tongue between those chattering teeth. Use Bruce Lee-style 'mind over matter' thinking to deflate those goosebumps and thaw that frostbite. Just like them fellas who walk over hot coals, Northerners have an ability to make their bodies do amazing things. When the Northern body says, 'I'm cold, put some clothes on', the Northern mind says, 'Shut it, lightweight! Let's crack on to the next pub, shall we?'

Follow these steps and you'll be able to cross the Antarctic in bermuda shorts and an Hawaiian shirt. And when you waltz past Bear Grylls in his thermal survival gear, why not give him a hand putting his tent up.

HOW TO... MINE COAL

For thousands of years, coal mining was a way of life for families up and down the North before Einstein invented electric gas and put all the miners out of work.

But even though things have moved on, you can still see remnants of those old skills in today's modern Northern workforce. For example, middle managers still wear hard hats around the office, builders insist on eating lunch in total darkness, postmen ride donkeys, and doctors always carry a dead canary.

But it's not all fun, fun, fun. There's a serious side to mining too – so if you're going to attempt it, have a look at my how-to guide first to avoid embarrassing yourself or killing others.

TERMINOLOGY: A coal mine and the surrounding structures are called 'a colliery'. This is not to be confused with 'a collie'. Or 'Norman Collier'.

Don't take a pick axe to a collie or you'll get nobbled by the RSPCA. Likewise, don't try chipping away at Norman Collier. There is no royal society that protects him and it's just not a very nice thing to do.

Also, you want to meet and hang around with 'miners', and not 'minors'.

Get that one wrong and you'll have Operation Ore knocking on your door – they have nothing to do with mining and everything to do with your own special wing in Strangeways.

Finally, men who come home from a day's work with black faces are miners. Men who go to work with black on their faces are racists. You want to be one of the first sort.

THE RIGHT TOOLS FOR THE JOB:
The tool of choice for any discerning coal miner is the pickaxe. Do not be tempted to 'update' to a ball pin hammer or 'go large' with a plough; neither will work down the pit.

A sturdy hobnail boot is also essential. Wellies, Ugg boots and tan leather slip-ons with tassels are no use at all. A pair of gloves will come in handy as will a hard hat – but don't be over-eager to become Northern and don the flat cap for a spell down the mine. It won't help when subsidence causes a tunnel to collapse.

Finally, overalls are preferable to shellsuits due to the irritating habit nylon has of discharging static shocks and sparking mine-wide gas explosions.

GETTING DOWN TO IT: Northern men always look nervous in lifts. Once you've tried plunging 2,000 feet down a roughly cut mine shaft in a creaky baked bean tin held up by bell wire, you'll start to see why. But stay calm and take a deep breath. Do not attempt to smoke a tab, though – it's considered impolite when surrounded by explosive coal dust.

Once you've crawled along a dark little tunnel for ages and made it to the coal seam, lie down in the most uncomfortable pose you can find and then hack away awkwardly with your pickaxe for twelve hours. Whatever you've mined by midday, you can eat for lunch, then it's another twelve-hour shift before collecting your thruppence wage and going home. It really is as simple as that!

Now you're a competent miner, why not try your hand at the much more lucrative excavation of diamonds, pearls and computer chips? It can't be that hard.

HOW TO... SMOKE A PIPE

CECI N'EST PAS UNE PIPE

This is a pipe. It's for smoking. Dave The Oracle says that gobbledegook writing below that picture above is actually foreign for, 'This is not a pipe'. But it obviously is a pipe – and quite a good one – which is why I've chosen it

to show you what a pipe looks like.

So now you know what a pipe is, here's how to use it.

THE LOOK: Pipes are not for the weak-hearted. I mean that in both a metaphorical sense (they're quite difficult to master) and a literal sense (they're really, really bad for you if you have a weak heart). That old showbusiness adage rings true here: never work with children or animals or make them smoke pipes. This is man's business. Specifically, three types of man:

A. The dandy
Dandies do things like eat caviar, play polo and wear monocles. There is no one of that description up here in the North, so we can disregard them for now.

B. The Sea-Dog
This is much more Northern. Please note, you don't have to have been in the Navy to fit this category, you just need to have been doing some sort of hard labour based on ships (e.g. merchant navy, fisherman). Plus a proper beard.

C. Einstein
This is an admittedly small category. A category of one, to be precise. If the cleverest man in the world

smoked a pipe, there must be something in it. Well, obviously there's tobacco in it, but you know what I mean.

No one else can smoke a pipe without looking ridiculous – and that includes footballers, students, pop stars, policemen and joggers.

THE TOBACCO: Pipes are made to smoke tobacco – and definitely not your crack weed or banana skins or moss or coal. Pipe tobacco looks a lot like the inside of cigarettes, except it comes in little packets or tins. And, unlike cigarettes which just taste of chemicals, pipe tobacco tastes of apples or cherries or whisky or vanilla – as well as chemicals.

Don't try and smoke it all at once – just pinch a little bit and put it in the end of the pipe. The big end, not the little end.

Also, don't try and light your pipe off someone else's pipe, the gas hob, the toaster or a bonfire. Trust me, those methods don't work.

THE TIMING: Smoke a pipe to celebrate a significant achievement, like circumnavigating the globe, climbing Everest or watching , *Under Siege* AND *Under Siege 2* back-to-back in one go. You can also smoke a pipe to hold people's attention – like when you're deliberating over the identity of a murderer at the end of a film, or deciding whether or not to abandon

ship at sea. Although, if you're on an aeroplane, in a petrol station or under the covers after a bit of you-know-what with the missus, that's not the time to spark up a pipe – even if you are deliberating over the identity of a murderer at the same time.

And that's all you need to know to smoke a pipe. So consider all of the above before you become a pipe smoker. On the negative side, they're filthy, they're antisocial and they give you lung cancer. On the positive side, they make you look clever. Hey, it worked for Einstein and Sherlock Holmes.

TV GUIDE

A lot of telly gets made down south because:

a) *That's where the major channels and studios are based.*

b) *That is also where the secret cabal of southern elitist TV executives who are intent on destroying Northern Britain is based. (Of course, with the exception of anyone who gives me work or works with me, they're exempt.)*

But since I've got my own book now, I thought I might use it as a platform to tell them London telly people what us Northerners really want to watch. So here is what the schedules would be like if I was the Director General of Telly.

Please don't be shocked that I have listed three channels here. I know exactly what you're thinking: 'Three channels! Not every Northerner has tuned into BBC 2 yet, you know!' Well, I've included it anyway just for those of you whizz kids who might have the technical know-how and arty leanings to have tuned it into your telly.

BBC 1

7.00 TOP OF THE POPS
Tonight's line-up includes Oasis, The Stone Roses, The Happy Mondays, The Smiths, The Beatles (all the ones that are left, anyway), Take That, The Verve and Joy Division (all the ones that are left, anyway) and definitely not The Pet Shop Boys.

8.00 NORTHENDERS
New Series. Soap focusing on Albert Square, Bolton. EastEnders has moved North, but with an entirely new, and Northern, cast. And it's not as depressing. And Ken Barlow's in it. I'll be straight with you, it's Coronation Street.

8.30 TOMORROW'S WORLD
Live from Barnsley. Tonight's show looks at new technology which will enable us to listen to cassette tapes while on the move. Also, an inventor who has created a device for cars which lights cigarettes (and no, it isn't just a box of matches), and a sneak peak at the latest video game to hit Northern electrical stores, 'Tetris'.

9.00 DAVID ATTENBOROUGH'S ESSEX
A natural history documentary following wildlife in the nightclubs of Essex. Sir David offers us an insight into the bizarre mating rituals of the indigenous species. Tonight's episode focuses on the males attaching spoilers on the back of their Ford Escorts.

10.00 MOVIE PREMIER – KES 2
In the sequel to the classic 1970 film, young Billy is all grown up. He's still a working-class Yorkshire lad, but now he's progressed from training kestrels to taming ostriches. Starring Bernie Clifton as Billy and Steven Seagal as Mr Sugden.

12.00 BBC 1's GENTLEMAN'S TEN-MINUTE FREEVIEW
A ten-minute preview of BBC 1's late-night phone-in. This is only available to Premium Adult TV Licence Holders (available via the internet and costs a tenner on top of your normal licence fee). BBC 1's sexiest ladies, including Arlene Phillips, Babs Windsor and Claire Balding, will be taking your suggestive calls from midnight.

12.10 CLOSEDOWN
That's all your BBC 1 for tonight, unless, of course, you've subscribed to the mucky stuff.

7.00 DARTS WORLD CHAMPIONSHIP
The sport of kings. The pastime of heroes. The game of gods. The recreation of stars. The activity of champions. Live action from the biggest sporting event on the planet. Who will win? Well, Phil 'The Power' Taylor will. But WHO will come second?

8.00 GEORDIEWATCH
Bill Oddie observes the birds out on the toon from his specially designed hide, which resembles a wheelie-bin. Tonight, Bill hopes to locate Geordie birds taking part in a 'Hen Night' – a ritual which begins with some frenetic dancing manoeuvres, but usually ends in a fight.

9.00 BEING CHUBBY
Documentary focusing on the life and legacy of high-brow comedian Roy Chubby Brown. Includes his early days of going to Edinburgh as part of the Cambridge Footlights, his French-speaking gigs in 1970s Paris, the Nobel Peace Prize he won for his tireless efforts to stop civil war in Rwanda, and the making of his 1993 arthouse film, and winner of the Cannes Jury Prize, U.F.O. Narrated by Sir Ian McKellen.

10.00 C.I.
Or 'Chuffing Interesting' to give the programme its full title. Hosted by Jim Bowen, the greatest and wittiest Northern minds discuss trivia about stuff that's chuffing interesting. Guests include Fred The Weatherman, Russ Abbott, Bobby Knutt and Jimmy Krankie.

11.00 NEWSNIGHT REVIEW
Tonight's panel will be discussing the BFI's upcoming retrospective season, 'Seagal: Auteur, Visionary and Hard Bastard', as well as reviewing the new Fast & Furious film and this year's Shoot Annual. Panel members include Cheryl Cole, Peter Andre and Nicola McClean.

12.00 BBC 2's GENTLEMAN'S TEN-MINUTE FREEVIEW
Spin-off from the BBC 1 show, this late-night phone-in features the female stars not of BBC 1, but the high-brow classy ladies of BBC 2 accepting your bawdy calls. Presented by Kirsty Wark, Deborah Meaden and Delia Smith.

12.10 CLOSEDOWN/MUCKY STUFF IF YOU'VE PAID EXTRA

7.00 UEFA CHAMPIONS LEAGUE FINAL LIVE
Tonight's final sees Real Madrid take on the biggest club in Europe, Bolton Wanderers FC. By an amazing coincidence, this year's Final venue is the Reebok Stadium, Bolton – so there should be a good home crowd. There will be even more spice in this tie with Real facing their former player, and now Bolton captain, Cristiano Ronaldo (who Bolton only signed when he promised to get a man's haircut and stop falling over like a little girl).

9.00 TAKE ME OUT – CELEBRITY SPECIAL
Celebrities looking for a date on this celebrity special include Brad Pitt, Leonardo DiCaprio, Tom Cruise and David Beckham. Among the celeb girls still waiting to be picked are Megan Fox, Beyonce and Susan Boyle. Hosted by the hilarious and charming Paddy McGuinness. Even in this international A-List company, McGuinness still stands head and shoulders above the rest.

10.00 UEFA CHAMPIONS LEAGUE FINAL HIGHLIGHTS
The highlights from Bolton's 8–0 thrashing of Real Madrid. Another chance to see Ronaldo's hat trick and Kevin Davies's five-goal haul.

11.00 MOVIE: ON DEADLY GROUND (1994)
Starring Steven Seagal and Michael Caine. Fifteen years before Al Gore started trying to save the world, Seagal was already protecting the Alaskan wilderness and its indigenous people. Seagal's pioneering movie finally gets the credit it deserves for helping to stop global warming. The film is preceded by a two-minute introduction by Barack Obama, in which he thanks Seagal for saving us all from certain death.

12.00 GOD'S GIFT (rpt)
Classic episode of the nineties dating show. Hosted by Davina McCall and Claudia Winkleman. Contestants include a buff-looking lad from Bolton named Master P. McGuinness breaking blocks of wood.

12.30 GRANADA'S GENTLEMAN'S TEN-MINUTE FREEVIEW
This late-night phone-in features female stars from your local region. They will be taking your risqué phone calls. Presented by The Loose Women.

12.40 CLOSEDOWN/MUCKY STUFF

GREAT NORTHERN
·*Women*·

JO GUEST

Born on 22nd February 1972 in Chesterfield, Jo Guest is a true Northern icon. Hardworking and feisty, she soon outgrew her modest Derbyshire roots and wanted more from life. She'd barely turned eighteen when, like a moth to a flame, Jo was drawn to the bright lights and glamour of catering college.

But it was halfway through a spotted dick in 1993 that Jo's broader appeal was realised and she got invited to appear in the hallowed pages of the Sun thanks to her two biggest assets – her charm and her business brain. Dispensing wisdom beyond her years, she dominated the pages of the UK's biggest newspaper for more than five years – which is a lot longer than Gordon Brown'll manage.

Jo herself had this to say:

How wrong she was about the acting. Because in 1995, she took Hollywood by storm with a powerful, driven performance as 'Police Woman' in the celebrated gangster flick *Hell to Pay*. Bolton Betamax Rentals haven't got *Hell to Pay* in yet, but if it's anything like Steven Seagal's *Under Siege* – and from the sound of the title, it is – then I'm sure it's brilliant.

> '*I thought to myself,*
> "*I can't sing and I can't act*
> *so I'll just be a Page 3 girl*".'
>
> INTERNATIONAL EXPRESS

Lumley's work is nothing compared to Jo's unselfish campaigning work for watercress. As early as 2003, Jo quipped:

'I'm proud to be launching the British watercress season. It's a really healthy little plant and it has a nice hot bite to it too. It's also said to be an aphrodisiac so I just can't get enough of it!'

THE MID & WEST HAMPSHIRE
OBSERVER, MAY 2003

Jo's selfless support of watercress is typical of her caring, sensitive nature. Who else but Jo would stand up for the semi-aquatic perennial leaf vegetable.

The last few years have seen a more mature, shy and reflective Jo shunning the spotlight. But the good news is she's back on our tellies – with her own seven-hour show every Friday night on something called channel 917. I think that's among the religious channels on Sky.

Whatever the future holds for this bright star, we salute her. Jo's drive and ambition are an inspiration to women everywhere. The North is proud.

Jo achieved all of this – plus being awarded the prestigious title of Miss Presto Cutting Tools 1994 – by the age of twenty-three. But her meteoric rise didn't stop there. For the next two years she offered *Daily Star* readers help and advice in all aspects of life as the newspaper's agony aunt. Or, as they called her, 'agony babe', presumably because she was still quite young.

The turn of the millennium saw the wholesome Jo embark on a brand-new venture. I believe it was her wish to touch every man in Britain – and the canny Jo knew how much her fans loved to use the internet. Which is why she began hosting her own show on the internet radio station Storm. Her heady mix of music and chat certainly touched me.

Jo's tireless promotion of an active, healthy lifestyle soon forced the DJ-ing to take a back seat. And forget Joanna Lumley and the Gurkhas.

time to appear in the kids' reality show *Byker Grove*, a shocking exposé on an east-Newcastle youth club that showed what it was really like growing up alongside Ant & Dec.

But whereas Ant & Dec went on to become the undisputed King and King of television, Donna's wide-ranging talents led her to cut a more zig-zaggy sort of path through showbusiness – and indeed life.

∽ DONNA AIR ∾

Donna Air was born in Geordieland on 2nd August 1979 – which makes her the same age as me, give or take. Don't bother checking that, there's no need, is there?

She did nothing until the age of ten, when she suddenly learned how to walk, talk and dress herself just in

Five years after bursting on to our screens, and still aged ten, Donna graduated from *Byker Grove* with a 2:1 and immediately forged a pop career with an all-girl group called 'Byker Grooove!' How she came up with that name we'll never know. In a bid to set themselves apart from every other band in history, Byker Grooove! released just one single – 1994's 'Love Your Sexy...!!' – which rocketed into the charts at number 48.

Not wanting the Byker Grooove! sound to go stale, Donna immediately disbanded them. Having found life in an all-girl pop group too stifling, Donna's next move was to form the all-girl pop group 'Crush'. In 1996, Crush exploded into the charts with 'Jellyhead', a Northern anthem with a sound rarely heard outside of Byker Grooove! The year 1996 was a time of upheaval in the North, and thank God that Donna was there to capture the mood so perfectly, with hauntingly beautiful lyrics that Sir Paul McCartney would be proud of:

'Over and over I feel it, boyfriend you're alone

~x~

You must be out of your mind, jellyhead

~x~

You've really blown it!'

LYRICS FROM 'JELLYHEAD'

The cassettes flew off the shelves and the single rocketed up the charts to number 50. Bowing to pressure from their fan, Crush followed up the single with an album – but Donna's record company knew the UK wasn't ready for such a fresh sound so they only released it abroad. After toiling away in the studio for almost a year, Crush released their difficult second album which they gave the very self-referential and postmodern title, 'Crush'. Typically for Donna, the album defied expectation by having all the same tracks on as the first album, just remixed and put in a different order. That's the kind of punk rock trick that only performance art talents such as Bill Drummond and Jimmy Cauty

would normally dare to attempt.

Sadly for music aficionados the world over, that marked an end to Donna's music career. Her spiritual home was telly and she turned her considerable talents to presenting instead. Her CV reads like a BAFTA 'Best Programme Ever' shortlist: *Gorilla Gorilla, Lynx Extended Play, Banged Up With Beadle, Donnaworld, Popgun, Apocalypse Tube, 50 Ways To Tease Your Lover, Donna In Need...* the list goes on. Every single one a smash. It's the mark of a true Northern lass to celebrate success but not go on about it, and that's why Donna's decided not to release any of her shows on VHS.

Of course, her creative work is all well and good but a lot of men just love Donna for her willingness to get down and dirty for the glossy mags. I am of course referring to her continuing work with the Soil Association and her photo-shoots for Certification News, the Soil Association's quarterly update about soil.

What's next? Is there anything left that this hard-working Northern lass hasn't already done? I don't know, but she's a true Northern ambassador. Donna Air – musician, pop star, band member, singer, vocalist, performer, presenter and soil fan – the North salutes you.

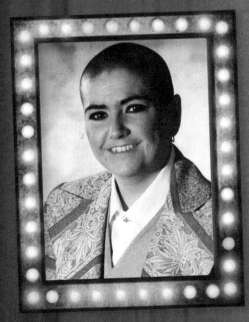

HUFFTY FROM THE WORD

with the details of where, how and when she grew up. Of course all of this information has been written about a million times, so I won't go into it here. Should you want to know more, just head to the Huffty section of your local library and wade through the volumes of historical information about the TV presenter.

A lot has been written about this great Northern woman, and I don't mean to jump on the bandwagon. But a book about the treasures of the North just wouldn't be complete without mentioning the region's big superstar Huffty. These days Huffty is a household name, but back in the nineties she had to work very hard to make it big.

You would be hard pushed to tell from her accent, but Huffty was born in Newcastle. In order to understand her fully, you need to get to grips

Her real name is 'Huffty from *The Word*' – but recently she changed it to Andrea Rea (probably after she married some lucky fella). The name Huffty was given to her by her parents in honour of her grandfather Lord William Huffty Walderidge-Smithe who was also an interviewer. He used to interview German detainees during the Second World War.

So what can I say about her childhood that hasn't already been written about? Well, she wasn't always the sex symbol that she is now. To my surprise I found out that, when she was at school, she was quite the tom-boy! But she was a trend-setter too. Some ten years before Britney was pushing the 'shaven headed' look, Huffty was already sporting it. This helped her stand out from the crowd... and simultaneously solved her nit problem.

In 1993 Huffty from *The Word* took a job on the popular TV series *The Word* where she learnt her trade from consummate professionals such as Terry Christian OBE and Dame Dani Behr. The moment she joined the team the whole nation sat up and listened. Who can forget her interview with that man in Australia whose mum they'd got in to talk to him about stuff 'n' that? Or that person she spoke about being at a Duran Duran concert or something? And then there was that time she interviewed that famous guy from

that action film... actually, forget that, that was Katie Puckrik. But Huffty had some great moments. She proved that not just anyone could present a TV programme.

In the mid-nineties, you could find Huffty pinned up on the wall of every red-blooded male's bedroom. That girl had a certain 'Je ne sais quoi'. The power of her beauty was so great that even women found her attractive.

She was, of course, the person who coined the phrase 'cushty'. Just imagine what the English language would be like without that word! It would be almost unrecognisable. She also invented the word 'canny' as in 'This song is canny good'. (Not to be confused with the Scottish word 'canny' as in 'I canny toss this caber, it's too heavy'.) *The Oxford English Dictionary* often invite her to write for them when they're struggling to come up with new words.

As time went on, Huffty built up a body of work that we're all extremely familiar with. Today she's known for one thing, and one thing only... and that's doing what she does best! She truly excels in her field. And the work she does in that field can only be described as 'indescribable'. She is a force unto her own. And her legacy will live on in the immense catalogue of work that she continues to present us with. That is why her name will never be erased from history. It will echo in the memory of a nation for eternity! We will never forget – Huffty! (Note to editor – Could someone check if Huffty's name is spelt with one f or two?)

NORTHERN GUIDE TO

ART

There are a lot of different opinions on what is and what isn't art. Just to clear it up once and for all, here's a list to help you spot if something's art or not.

A painting: That IS art.

A drawing: That IS art.

A sculpture: That IS art.

Putting any old shit in a room: That is NOT art! It's a piss-take.

A photograph: NO! That is NOT art! At best it's a holiday snap.

A photograph of a nude lady: That IS art. But I'd class it as specialist art.

Cutting animals in half: NO! That is NOT art! That's butchering. And butchering is what butchers do, not bloody artists.

So I hope that's finally sorted that out then. Let's hear no more debates about the nature of art.

Of course art couldn't exist if it wasn't for the artists. Here are the key players in art:

Leonardo Da Vinci Code

Leonardo Da Vinci is not just a character played by Tom Hanks. No, he was a real-life artist. I assume he did most of his drawings when he wasn't solving crimes. He is best known for his painting 'The Mona Lisa's Smile', which was also turned into a film starring Bob Hoskins.

Rolf Harris

Rolf started painting a few years after the Da Vinci Code. He mainly specialises in drawing rare animals (such as the Rolf-a-Roo) and using a wobbly board.

Tracy Emin

Dunno what she paints pictures of. But any girl that's been drunk on national television gets my vote.

Morph

Morph was such a passionate artist that he even slept with his brushes. But he rarely got the chance to paint because Chas (damn that bloody Chas) would always steal his equipment. Sadly, any paintings he did do were usually too small to see.

Now you know the artists, it's time to teach you about the most important pieces of art in history. Here's my run-down of top art:

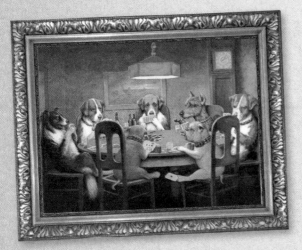

DOGS PLAYING POKER

BY UNKNOWN

Can't remember if this is one is by Leonardo or Rolf, but it's flippin' brilliant anyway. Just imagine having the sort of mind that could dream up dogs playing poker. It beggars belief. The man's a genius.

Take your time when looking at this picture. Don't just glance at it. Think. A painting like this evokes many a question – like 'When he got those dogs to pose for him, did he glue the cards and chips to their paws?', 'Could I train my dog to smoke a cigar?' and 'What would a dog think about Dave "Devilfish" Ulliott www.pokerpages.com/player-profile/dave-ulliott.htm?' If you happen to know the answer to any of these questions, please let me know as they are keeping me awake at night. His other masterpieces include dogs playing snooker and dancing. Personally I think that's choosing between beer and cider. You just can't improve on dogs playing poker. What an artist. Incredible.

WOMAN SCRATCHING HER BUM

BY ATHENA

The first thing that strikes you when you look at this picture is that she's not wearing any knicky-knacks. The second thing that strikes you is that she must have an itchy bum. The third thing that strikes you is that she's not wearing any knicky-knacks. It's very noticeable.

Funnily enough, most of my women friends don't like this picture as much as me. I've spent a lot of time thinking about why this might be. Why would men like it more than women? I reckon it's because men are more into sport than women. It's that or they've noticed that no one's playing tennis with her – so they think it's a very sad picture.

It's a very clever photo because it immediately draws your eye in, to particular parts of it anyway. It evokes a lot of emotions when you look at it. To begin with you feel a bit sexy, but the more you look at it the more you wonder if, perhaps, it could be a man in a dress. I mean, she could have a todger and a beard. Once that image is in your head, it's very hard to shake it. It makes you feel strange. So whatever you do, don't think about that. The only other Athena works worthy of mention would be muscular man holding a baby and muscular man holding car tyres.

THE (UNOFFICIAL) STEVEN SEAGAL CALENDAR 1995

BY STEVEN SEAGAL

Now this is what I call art. The (Unofficial) Steven Seagal Calendar 1995 is like a portable art gallery. Every page contains a work that would make even Brian Sewell cry. Plus, it was only £1.98 from Woolies! Compare that to the million quid you'd have to pay to get Jackson Pollack to chuck a couple of tins of Dulux at a wall and… well… you don't have to be Stephen Hawking to work out that the Seagal Calendar is good value for money.

If I had to pick one thing about the calendar that I thought was brilliant, I'd have to say it's the fact that he's holding guns.

But don't worry if guns are not your thing. There's also a picture of him holding knives. Seagal caters for everyone.

Just look at March, Seagal's eyes seem to follow you around the room. It's as if he's trying to tell you something like, 'I'm just a cook', or 'Die you terrorist cock sucker'.

What really blows you away with this piece is he's signed EVERY page. How he found the time I'll never know. He's even put down messages for you on each page. For example, on one page it says 'Merry Christmas! From Steven Seagal'. Unfortunately that page is 'July'. Must have been a printing error.

THREE FLYING DUCKS
(SCULPTURE)

BY POUNDLAND

First seen on the walls of a certain Mrs Ogden of Corry Street. This piece is extremely versatile – you can shove it up in the living room or you can shove it outside by the front door – you can start with the smallest duck on the left or the right – the choices are endless.

Just like Mona Lisa's Smile, there is a mystery to the Three Flying Ducks that has puzzled scholars for years: Are they flying to a lake or from a lake? In truth, we'll never know. But as with all art, you get out of it what you put into it. Talking of putting stuff in, when you buy this piece you have to provide your own nails.

The one thing you can be sure of – if you put these little fellas up in your house, then everyone will know you're an art boffin. So why not stop reading this and pop down your local art store (Poundland/Ikea) and grab yourself three flying ducks.

And don't worry; art like this will never go out of fashion.

NORTHERN THEORY TEST

Just because you come from Burnley, Billingham or Brampton, it doesn't automatically make you a Northerner. Things aren't that easy. It's a little known fact outside of the North that every man, woman and child must first pass the NTT (Northern Theory Test) before they can legally call themselves a Northerner, drink mild, or complain about the weather. Northern Law Statutes are very specific on the etiquette:

Like the Masons or the Bolton Brewers Real Ale Society, the details surrounding the NTT and inauguration into the Northern Fraternity are cloaked in mystery. But here, for the first time in print, are the actual questions from the NTT. They've never been seen before south of Chester, so this is a rare opportunity to see how you do at being Northern...

'Only upon achieving a pass grade in the Northern Theory Test may a successful candidate be permitted to refer to themselves as "Northern" or "a Northerner". Furthermore, all other Northerners must cease to use the title "that" and instead employ "our" when referring to the candidate; i.e. "that Terry Nutkins" becomes "our Terry Nutkins".'

Northern Law Statute 3a

NORTHERN THEORY TEST

VER.6
16 HOURS

[Answer ALL questions in the space provided.
Smoking breaks permitted only at minute intervals.]

QUESTION 1
Who is the most famous Northerner?

QUESTION 2
What's a typical Northern dish?

QUESTION 3
How many people live in the North?

QUESTION 4
What is the correct greeting in Northern polite society?

QUESTION 5
Where might you see the following flag?

QUESTION 6
What's the most offensive gesture to a Northerner?

QUESTION 7
James Hargreaves invented the spinning jenny one afternoon in 1764 and is widely credited with starting the Industrial Revolution. But what was the name of the period that followed?

QUESTION 8
Whilst driving you see the following sign; what should you do?

QUESTION 9
Scotland is part of the North. True or false?

QUESTION 10
How does a Geordie spell 'Northern'?

QUESTION 11
How far is Holmfirth from London?

QUESTION 12
What is mined from Pendle Hill Pit in Lancashire?

ONCE YOU'VE ANSWERED ALL THE QUESTIONS, ATTRACT THE LANDLORD'S ATTENTION AND HAND OVER YOUR SHEET AND CRAYON PLUS TEN POUNDS 'PERSUASION' FEE.

THIS IS THE END OF THE PAPER

Q1 Anton Dec. **Q2** Will accept Lancashire hotpot, anything with a pie crust or Bet Lynch. **Q3** Plenty cocker. **Q4** Trick question; there's no such thing as polite society in the North. It's a firm handshake, a smile and a slap on the back. **Q5** London. **Q6** No more drink for me, thanks. **Q7** Dinner time. **Q8** Stop, turn around and go back the way you came; you're in danger of entering the south (or Harrogate) where costs rise steeply. **Q9** False. Unless a Scotsman is within earshot, in which case it's true. **Q10** The same as everyone else; they're not stupid! **Q11** It feels like a million miles away. **Q12** Northern Grit.

215

*My love & thanks to
Christine, Leah, Dad plus all my
family & friends. Without you
lot I'd be lost.*

Endpaper map illustrations © Claire Littlejohn

Picture Acknowledgements

© Alamy: 3 (bottom left), 4 (middle & bottom), 8 (left), 10 (top left), 11 (top left), 12 (top left & top right), 15 (top), 20 (top), 26 (top), 28, 29 (top), 36 (middle left), 37 (bottom right), 38 (top right), 39 (middle right & bottom), 40 (top right & left, bottom left), 49 (left), 50 (right), 59 (top left), 62, 64 (top), 65, 67 (right), 69 (top), 73, 78 (bottom), 79 (left), 80, 81, 82, 83 (top right & bottom left), 84 (bottom), 90, 93 (top), 111 (bottom), 114 (middle left), 121 (bottom left), 126 (top right), 129, 131 (middle right), 132, 133 (top, middle right & bottom), 137 (left), 147, 148, 151 (top & bottom), 153, 156, 157, 168 (top right), 172, 196 (bottom), 209, 211 (top), 212, 213. © Ardea: 68 (left)/photo Pat Morris. © BIGPICTURES.COM: 179, 189. Harry Potter and the Philosopher's Stone by J.K. Rowling © Bloomsbury Publishing Plc: 125. © The Bolton News and Bury Times: 108-109 (middle), 110. Journey Under The Sea by R.A. Montgomery © 2010 Chooseco LLC, Waitsfield VT: 126. © Corbis: 3 (bottom right), 10 (top right), 23 (right), 30 (right), 75 (top), 89, 185. © Photographer Martin Elliott (who licensed Athena to publish in poster form 1976-1995): 211. © Getty Images: 8 (bottom right), 9 (top & bottom left), 11 (top right), 12 (middle right & bottom right), 20 (bottom), 21, 39 (left), 48 (top right), 83 (bottom right), 130, 131 (top), 150, 155 (top), 168 (middle, middle left & bottom), 186, 188. © Kobal Collection/Warner Bros/Regency: 87. Our Friends, The Ladybird Key Words Reading Scheme by William Murray © Ladybird Books Ltd, 1964: 124. © Matrixphotos.com: 182 (bottom), 187. © Press Association Images: 11 (bottom right), 103 (left), 127. Personal collection: 139 (top). Courtesy Phil McIntyre Entertainment Ltd: 84 (top), 128 (top), 170 (top left). © Photolibrary.com: 3 (top & left), 8 (middle right), 9 (top right), 38 (bottom right). © Photoshot: 63 (top right)/photo World Pictures, 79 (right)/photo Imagebrokers. © Reuters: 183. © Rex Features: 11 (bottom left), 16, 17 (top), 18, 22, 24 (top), 26 (bottom), 27, 30 (left), 31, 37 (top right), 38 (bottom left), 39 (top), 40 (bottom), 41 (bottom left & right), 63 (left), 64 (bottom), 66 (top), 67 (left), 68 (right), 71 (top), 72, 75 (bottom), 78 (top), 88, 91, 94, 98, 100 (middle), 101, 102 (right), 104, 106, 112 (right), 113, 114 (top, middle right, bottom), 115 (top), 131 (middle left), 146, 152, 154, 155 (bottom), 160 (top), 168 (top left), 173, 174, 175, 176, 177, 178, 180, 181, 182 (top), 184, 204, 205, 206, 207, 208, 210. Courtesy Warburtons Ltd: 69.

Every reasonable effort has been made to contact the copyright holders, but if there are any errors or omissions, Hodder & Stoughton will be pleased to insert the appropriate acknowledgement in any subsequent printing of this publication.

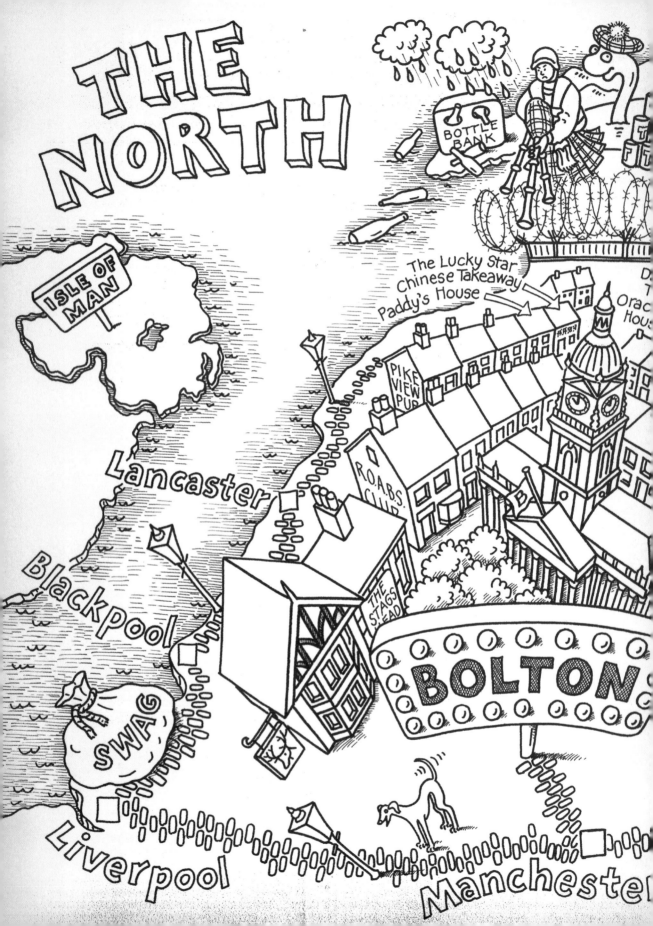

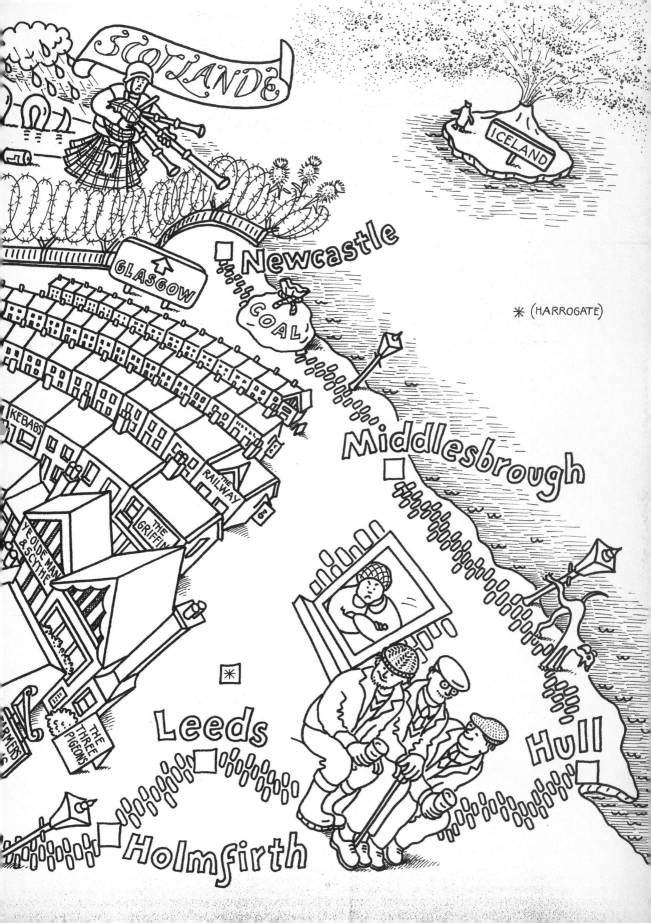